The Rise and Fall… and Rise Again

The Rise and Fall... and Rise Again

By Gerald Ratner

CAPSTONE
be inspired! ™

John Wiley & Sons, Ltd

Other Wiley Editorial Offices

John Wiley and Sons Inc., 111 River Street, Hoboken, NJ 07030, USA
Jossey-Bass, 989 Market Street, San Francisco, CA 94103-1741, USA
Wiley-VCH Verlag GmbH, Boschstr. 12, D-69469 Weinheim, Germany
John Wiley and Sons Australia Ltd, 42 McDougall Street, Milton, Queensland 4064, Australia
John Wiley and Sons (Asia) Pte Ltd, 2 Clementi Loop #02-01, Jin Xing Distripark, Singapore 129809
John Wiley & Sons Canada Ltd, 6045 Freemont Blvd, Mississauga, ONT, L5R 4J3, Canada

Wiley also publishes its books in a variety of electronic formats. Some content that appears in print may not be available in electronic books.

Anniversary Logo Design: Richard J. Pacifico

A catalogue record for this book is available from the British Library and the Library of Congress.

ISBN 13: 978-1-84112-786-6

Typeset in 11/15.5 pt Berkeley by Thomson Digital
Printed and bound in Great Britain by TJ International Ltd, Padstow, Cornwall

This book is printed on acid-free paper responsibly manufactured from sustainable forestry in which at least two trees are planted for each one used for paper production.

Substantial discounts on bulk quantities of Capstone Books are available to corporations, professional associations and other organizations. For details telephone John Wiley & Sons on (+44) 1243-770441, fax (+44) 1243 770571 or email corporatedevelopment@wiley.co.uk

For Moira, Suzy, Lisa, Sarah, Jonny and Alfie, my dog

Contents

Introduction

In 2006, a book was published called *History's Worst Decisions*. Alongside Nero burning Rome to the ground, Eve eating the apple, and the choice not to install a Tsunami warning system in the Indian Ocean, was a speech that I made in 1991. Despite the fact that I didn't kill anybody, I didn't do anything illegal, and I didn't even say anything that I hadn't said before, that speech caused me to lose my business, my reputation, and my fortune. The cost of most people's mistakes can't be so precisely measured, and I think the reason my story keeps turning up in these lists is that my losses can be quantified. It says something about our society that people like to know what I lost in monetary terms: a £650,000 salary, £500 million wiped off the valuation of my company, and a billion pound turnover slashed virtually overnight.

In the weeks and months immediately after the speech, my life changed almost seismically. I kept thinking that it would soon be over and that people would forget about the speech, that they'd stop calling me Mr Crapner, and that the phrase 'Doing a Ratner' would disappear. I was wrong: if you Google me, which I confess to having done (who hasn't?), the first result is a Wikipedia entry on 'Doing a Ratner'. Even though my name had once been above hundreds of shops up and down the country, it had become more famous as a byword for crap.

It took several years to realise what an impact the speech has had on every aspect of my life – emotionally and socially, as well as financially. I didn't know it at the time, but it turned out to be the most significant moment of my life, and it now casts a strange light over everything that led up to it, and everything that's stemmed from it. As I've written this book, I've noticed that it's crept onto many of the pages, either directly, or as a figure in the shadows, waiting to make its entrance.

It's not nice to be known for just one thing – I imagine, even if that's a wonderful thing like winning an Olympic medal, as we are all more complex than the headlines let on. But when the thing you're known for is a negative thing, a stupid thing, a thing that only lasted 30 minutes, you start to resent it. Especially as in the years since, so much has been written about it that is inaccurate. These days, I do a lot of public speaking, and when I tell my audiences that I never said my jewellery was crap, they are surprised, if not amazed.

It's now been 16 years since that speech, and from time to time journalists ask me if I regret it. Well of course I bloody regret it! Who wouldn't? However, as time has gone on, I've started to appreciate what it has given me: as Frank Sinatra knew, comebacks are a lot of fun.

ACT I

The Rise

CHAPTER I

Family Life

My father opened his first jewellery shop in 1949, which also happens to be the year I was born, and as my mother worked in the shop while she was pregnant with me, I think I can claim to have been born into the jewellery trade. It is in my blood, and that makes it almost impossible to talk about my family and childhood without also talking about the business – in my mind the two things are inseparable. And that, of course, is what made losing the business all those years later so much harder. I didn't just lose my job, I lost the only job I'd ever had, and the only job I'd ever wanted. If you've never worked in a family business, it can be hard to understand, but I loved the business like it was part of the family, and in some ways the business was a bit like having a third parent or an extra sibling.

My parents had met in India during the war, when my father Leslie was stationed there. On Fridays, local Jewish families invited Jewish soldiers to participate in the Sabbath with them. One of those families was my grandmother's. She had fled to Bangalore from Iraq with her 11 children to escape persecution of Jews after a coup had brought a pro-Nazi leader to power. Call me cynical, but I'm pretty sure my father was invited with the sole intention that my grandmother would be able to marry off one of her daughters, and as it happened my father fell hook, line, and sinker for her eldest, Rachelle. He was a very impulsive man, and the fact that my mother had a daughter from a previous marriage didn't deter him at all.

My parents were to remain utterly devoted to each other for the next five decades, but their marriage caused friction between my father and his family. When he returned to their house in St Albans after the war, they were appalled.

'What have you done?' they asked. 'Not only is she divorced, but she's not even English!'

They turned him away, and from that day on, my father never got on with my grandfather again. It wasn't much of a welcome home for a returning soldier, and my mother was left in no doubt about what her in-laws thought of her. I'm sure this made my parents even closer.

While he'd been in India, a friend had given my father some Persian carpets to sell as they'd fetch a better price in England. He used to tell me he was demobbed with 10 shillings and a packet of cigarettes, so he was very motivated to get a good price for these carpets. He went round to my grandfather's rich neighbours with the rugs on his shoulder, selling them door to door. By all accounts they were amazing carpets, and when he got on his hands and knees and rolled them out, people had never seen anything like them. He was supposed to wire the money straight back to India, but with a wife and step-daughter to think of, he used the cash to open his first shop, which was in Richmond, West London. The fellow in India kept asking for the money, but my father kept stalling him until he had sufficient cashflow. It was very naughty of him, but I imagine that my mother was somewhere in the background, egging him on. She always told me that she was from a very good family, and I get the impression she was a bit shocked at her economic status in post-war London. At the time my parents were living in two rooms above a dental surgery in Richmond, down the road from the shop. Before long they'd be sharing those rooms with their first child together, my sister Juliet.

It could have been any kind of shop – I'm sure my father would have made a success of any trade he'd gone into – but he chose jewellery because his father had once been a watchmaker, so I guess he felt he had a bit of grounding in the industry. It wasn't a great business at first, but it paid the rent. A few months in though, he had a stroke of luck when one of his contacts supplied him with gold lockets from America that transformed his business. Lockets were hugely popular after the war, but the only place you could get them in West London was Ratners. As soon as the stock came in, it went out again. Then, just as now, a single line can turn a business around.

My half-sister Diane stayed in India until my parents could afford to support her, and by the time I was two, we had moved from the rooms above the dentist's to a detached house in Hendon. The business was expanding quickly, and Diane joined us not long after; and as my parents were so involved with the business, Diane practically raised me and Juliet.

I think it's fair to say that my mother really pushed my father. She had aspirations and spent a lot of money on things like mink coats and spin dryers that the neighbours would be impressed by. She used to borrow a lot of money too, and so my dad had to work even harder to pay the banks. She encouraged my dad to drive a Jaguar, albeit a second-hand one, because she wanted to show off. These days you need a yacht and a plane to show off, but not a lot of people had money in the Fifties, and if you had a fur coat and a spin dryer then your stock really went up, and that's what she wanted.

We usually ate as a family, even though my mother was a pretty lousy cook. All those years in India and all she'd learnt about spice was how to tip far too much curry powder into a stew! She really wasn't a woman suited to domestic chores, and found the business much more exciting. So whenever we sat down to a bland meal of meat and two veg, the conversation would inevitably turn to the business, which always made up for the spice lacking in the food.

At some point when I was quite young, my father had merged his shops into a business with his father Philip and brothers Jack and David, who also ran jewellery shops. They had a chain of about 13 when they joined forces, which gave them more purchasing power and streamlined overheads. Although my father was the major shareholder, my mother still felt Jack and my grandfather had too much say in how the company was run. As a young child, I sat at the table listening to the gossip about the business, how David had got the shop fittings wrong, or where they should open the next branch. It was quite clear that my mother thought my uncles and grandfather were a waste of space, so I learnt early on that running a family business always involves a fair amount of feuding. From about the age of 10 onwards, I was always asked for my opinion on things like who deserved promotion or what lines we should discontinue. I was so involved that I really felt like I was part of the company, even though I was still at school.

My father seemed to have the solutions to most problems, and I began looking up to him from a very early age. I absolutely adored him, and when I was taken to the shops I'd be so excited to see him that I would run into his arms. I worshipped him and even as a young child looked at him as a great success. He was a wonderfully kind man as well, and very generous to his family and staff. He started a scheme to let his managers borrow the deposit for a home so that they could get a mortgage, and this only added to the respect and loyalty he inspired. He really cared about everybody, and genuinely got upset if anyone was in difficulty. He had the most incredible personality; he only ever wanted to talk about you, and he encouraged all his family and his staff to do their best.

While all my parents' talk about the business inspired and excited me, looking back, I can see that it created problems too. In my young mind, I believed that the most important thing was to make money, and that to please my parents I had to be successful in business. It was drummed into me the whole time, and I was given examples of other people who were successful; they were called 'menches', people like Charles Clore and Isaac Wolfson who were the big successes of their day, and they were gods in our house. You didn't look up to a great poet or musician or writer in our house – they were not even mentioned – that's how focused the family was on business and wealth. That's not to say we were wealthy. We were not even particularly well off in comparison with some of our neighbours, and the arrival of my younger sister Denise in 1956 added to the monthly expenses.

When I got a bit older, I used to spend as much of my summers as I could at the Hendon Hall Hotel, where there was an open air swimming pool. All the local kids hung out there and I seemed to know everybody. I guess I showed a bit of early business promise by arranging to work there so I didn't have to buy a season ticket. I was only young – probably under 10 – but I worked the turnstiles and in the café. In those days, you used to get a penny for empty glass bottles, so I had a nice little sideline saying to the swimmers, 'Have you finished your drink? Let me take that away for you.' Those pennies added up, and I enjoyed having a bit of spending money.

One season I got the job of painting the swimming pool blue. I got a bit of paint on my shoes, and for some reason I thought it might show less if I painted the whole of my shoes and trousers blue too! My logic was that it would somehow be better and wouldn't look as bad. Needless to say, my parents never forgot when I returned back to the house for lunch completely covered in paint. They relayed that story to friends for years, often comparing it with a time when I had turned blue for real: according to my parents, when I was a baby I had been left in the garden in my pram during a thunderstorm and had been hit by lightning. By the time they remembered me, I had turned blue, but my father put me in a bath of warm water and I came back to life.

Each year, for 11 years running, the Ratners went on holiday on precisely August 15th, and we always went to Cannes. Lots of my father's friends went on holiday there, I guess because it was the place to be seen. I'd sit on the beach and look at movie stars like Terry Thomas, Tommy Steele, and Sophia Loren. It was incredibly exciting, but for the Ratners it was glamour on the cheap. My parents were careful not to pay for things like a sea view, and eventually they rented an apartment because it was more cost-effective. And my father worked out that the public beach was right next to the private one, so he asked the bus boys to set out his sun lounger right at the edge of the public beach so that you could kid yourself you were in with the in-crowd. Of course, I found it a bit embarrassing that my dad went to such lengths to save a few quid, but he let us order a Coca-Cola, and they would serve it in a glass with lemon and ice – this was in the early Sixties when we just didn't do that in England – and charge a franc for it, which was about 1s 6d, when a Coke back home only cost thruppence. But it didn't matter because they served it beautifully and we just used to sit there and watch the beautiful people. And at night I would hang out in the hotel lobby and look at couples who dressed up in their jewellery and finest clothes to go to the casino. My parents were one of those couples, and in the morning they would tell us who they had seen. Although the jewellery business was growing, my parents weren't rich by any means, but somehow they managed to have a glamorous lifestyle on a modest budget.

Despite the glamour, nothing ever seemed as exciting to me as my father's business. It was an adult world that I was endlessly curious about, and if I was ever bored and my mother asked what I would like to do, my answer was always to visit my father in one of his shops. When I eventually took over the business, we still had some of the managers from the early days, and a few of them found it odd having me as their boss. They'd say things like, 'I remember when your head didn't reach the top of the counter, are you sure about those figures?' Whenever my father let me, I would work in the shops running errands and delivering messages. They were some of the best days of my life.

CHAPTER 2
Growing Up

I think we can all look back on our lives and pinpoint moments when things changed. I have a very clear recollection of sitting on the stairs at our house in Hendon with my sisters. We were watching my mother's lips move as she told us that our father was about to have an operation.

'He's unlikely to survive', she told us.

Nobody else would say something like that to their children, but that was my mother – she just loved to say ridiculously outrageous things, even if it meant scaring her children so they wouldn't sleep. She knew how much I loved my father, and saying something like that was incredibly cruel, but she just said things the way she thought they were.

My father needed an operation to remove a tumour in his brain that was pressing on his optic nerve. It was a dangerous operation, but the odds were that he would survive surgery, despite what my mother had said, and as the tumour wasn't malignant, I discovered later that he should make a full recovery. When he came home from hospital, however, it was clear that he had changed. Not only was his head shaved, with a big U-shaped scar across the top, which was quite frightening on a man of 6′ 2″, but it gradually became clear that his personality had altered. Some people wouldn't have noticed, but compared with the person I knew, he had become much colder and he'd get easily frustrated, and that made him impossible and irrational.

In the first few weeks after he came home, he couldn't lie in bed because of a drip-line fed through his nose, and because I felt sorry for him I sat with him. I kept thinking it was just the operation, and that he'd be back to his old self soon, but it turned out that it was just the first of several operations on his brain, and his personality continued to harden over the next few years.

I was spared the worst of it. I remained his blue-eyed boy, but he was incredibly rude to my sisters, and my mother would lose her temper with him frequently. 'I'm never eating in a restaurant with him again!' she'd claim dramatically as they came in the door. We all knew why: he had become very argumentative. He would have rows with waiters and shop assistants and air stewardesses. At times he was so rude that it was almost funny.

'Look', he'd say, 'could you cut out all this chitchat and just serve me the meal?'

We were too nervous to laugh as people were frequently offended. But because he was successful, and was starting to have money to spend, people put up with him. In those days, if you were successful, you could get away with being rude. Years later, he would come for Sunday lunch at my house with my kids, and complain of feeling cold – he thought anything outside of London was draughty – and he'd get up from the table and fetch his hat and coat. He'd spend the rest of lunch in his hat and coat! He didn't mean it in a jokey way, which was a shame, because my kids thought it was hilarious.

It was like he had developed what people now call autism – we'd never heard of it in the Sixties – and of course it had a knock-on effect on the business. Key members of staff found him impossible to deal with, and his relationship with his brothers became increasingly fractious. For long periods at a time they refused to speak to each other, and only communicated through the company accountant, Mr Hussein.

'Mr Hussein, would you tell Jack to go to the Slough branch this afternoon.'

'Mr Hussein, would you tell Leslie to make sure he keeps his appointment with the wholesalers.'

It was even like this when they were in the same room as each other. It was an absolutely ridiculous situation, and at times they must have seemed like a dysfunctional family from a sitcom.

It affected all of us a great deal, and my performance at school started to nosedive. I had scraped through my Eleven Plus and had just started at Hendon County grammar school when my father got ill, and I found that most of what I was taught went right over my head. At my primary school, which was a small school in a house that had only four classes in it, I'd practically received one-to-one teaching. I was now in with 32 other kids and when the end of term reports came out, I had come 33rd out of 33. Looking back, I wonder if I'd had some kind of learning difficulty that was never diagnosed, because I just don't remember understanding any of it.

On the last day of term I went home with my report. I wasn't worried what my mother would say, because I was never scared of my mother: she would scream and shout, but there wouldn't be any real venom. It was my father I was worried about.

'Let's look at your report book then. What's it like?'

'It's terrible', I said honestly.

'It can't be that bad. Hand it over.'

He opened it up and saw it had 33 with a line and 33 underneath.

'You came bottom? You came last?'

I had always wanted to impress my father and I felt I had let him down. I came 33rd in the second term too, and Mr Potts my headmaster called my parents in to the school. Not only had I come bottom again, but in one exam – German – I'd got nought, which I think means I didn't even bother to put my name on the exam paper. He told them that if I came bottom in the third term then I would be asked to leave the school. He said he was particularly annoyed because my Eleven Plus had been borderline and he'd had to persuade the governors to let me in. That made me feel like I'd let everyone down, but it still wasn't enough for me to raise my grades.

My parents knew I wasn't stupid though, as I'd started studying for my bar mitzvah with a rabbi who came round to teach me each week. I had to learn about the Bible, the Old Testament obviously, and memorise some prayers in Hebrew that I had to sing in the synagogue. I learnt all of that perfectly well, and to this day, I know a hell of a lot more about the Bible than I know about chemistry or geography or anything like that. I'm pretty sure it's because I had one-to-one teaching, and my results at school were bad just because I couldn't cope in a large class.

Needless to say, I came 33rd in the third term as well and so I moved schools to Town and Country in Swiss Cottage, where I did equally badly. Being the new kid wasn't easy, especially as people soon learned why I had moved schools. I couldn't wait until I was old enough to leave.

There were just two things at school that I wasn't the worst in the class at – football and maths. I certainly wasn't great at football, but I enjoyed it and it bred in me a lifelong love of the game. I started going to Arsenal matches with my friends, and when we got a bit older, we followed them around Europe. In my teens, Arsenal became a major obsession and I can still remember the names of the entire 70/71 team. I can even remember the Spurs team from the Sixties.

To this day, I still have the head for maths that saved me from further embarrassment at school, and although I can't remember trigonometry or logarithms, I can multiply a three-digit number by another three-digit number almost instantly. In fact, this was my party trick when I was younger, and when we had guests, my parents got a calculator out and people would test me on random sums. I can still work out figures faster than any accountant I've worked with, but at school I could never seem to work out what the question was asking for. To put it simply, I was a complete and utter disaster at school.

Obviously this wasn't something I was pleased about, but I wasn't devastated about it either. These days, for my kids and their friends, grades and qualifications mean so much more, but in the Sixties it really wasn't that unusual to leave school without any qualifications. It certainly didn't mean you couldn't get a job, especially when your father ran a business that you were itching to get into. My parents gave my education one last chance by sending me to a cramming school, but that wasn't the answer either. One day I came home from school, clearly miserable, and my father recognised what a complete waste of time my education had become. I had just turned 15, which meant I could legally leave school.

'It's clear you want to work in the business and that you don't want to be at school', he said, 'so why don't you start with us full time?'

I'd been the Saturday boy at the Wood Green branch for a few years by then, and I'd loved it. So when my father said this to me, it was just about the best thing I'd ever heard. I left school without a single qualification, quite happily, and went to work behind the counter in the Oxford Street shop, one of the flagships of the ever-growing Ratners chain.

CHAPTER 3

Toughening Up

London was the centre of the universe in the Sixties, and my friends and I made the most of it. I was part of a big social scene, and every Saturday night without fail we would meet at 7 o'clock outside Golders Green Station, which was about 15 minutes on the bus from Hendon. About 150 kids would turn up and say 'Right, what are we doing tonight then?' Someone would always know about a party in Temple Fortune or a club on Tottenham Court Road. Then we all got on a bus – we behaved really quite badly, throwing things and shouting – and went off *en masse* for another great night. If there wasn't a party, then we'd go to the bowling alley and hang out there. You never knew where you'd end up until you got to Golders Green.

I used to spend quite a lot of money on clothes; I and a few friends would think nothing of going down to the West End to buy our Cuban heels in Anello and Davide, because that's where the Beatles bought their boots. I don't think I've ever had a bigger thrill in my life, not even making £100 million, than buying those Chelsea boots with my friends on a Saturday morning. We all bought exactly the same boots, and then went out in them that evening. We felt fantastic, not only were we that bit taller, but they were the thing to have and not everyone could afford them. We were flash, there's no other word for it, although my dad said I was turning into a 'spiv'. I used to walk along Golders Green Road in my Beatle boots, and for some reason there was a particularly cool way you had to wear your coat. It always had to be undone and your hands had to be in your pockets so the coat looked good. That was the way to walk, and so that was the way I made sure I was seen walking!

As far as I remember, none of us drank alcohol, although we all smoked. There was one kid who never touched cigarettes, so we gave him the nickname 'Smokey'. There was a fair bit of gambling too, and although every gambler tells you he wins, I'm pretty sure I made money playing Shoot Pontoon. I certainly got a reputation for being a tough opponent because I had the balls to shoot the whole bank, and most people were too scared to. Often I could make a couple of quid, and once, I remember, the bank was £7, and that seemed like a fortune when my pocket money was only 15 shillings. Perhaps not surprisingly, there were a few of us who were gambling mad, and who knows, perhaps it was this exposure to risk tolerance that helped a number of us become successful in business later on. One of my toughest opponents at Shoot Pontoon was Irving Scholar, who would go on to make a fortune in property and become the chairman of Tottenham Hotspur.

We went to some of the hippest clubs, including the Country Club in Belsize Park (where I met a relatively unknown band called the Rolling Stones and chatted to Mick Jagger for a couple of minutes), Beat City in Tottenham Court Road, and Whisky-A-Go-Go in Soho, but despite our sophistication I don't think any of us had ever done more than kiss a girl, and no one had a steady girlfriend. That was still a few years off, but nevertheless I was very confident and thought I was one of the coolest kids in London.

Occasionally, we'd get into fights. I don't know if it was because we were Jewish, but our parents always told us, 'Don't fight amongst yourselves', so we were very defensive of each other. You had to put across to people that you were hard – that was the word we used all the time – but as I was a bit on the young side to be in this social scene, there were always older people in the places we went to who were in a position to beat us up. It was quite terrifying, but it was all part of the excitement of the clubs and secretly we all loved the danger.

For a few years, my relationship with my friends was more important than my relationship with my family, even my father. I'd got to an age where I could see his flaws and the days of hero-worshipping him were long gone. I had two particular friends, Tommy and Eddie, who both lived in the flats on the Great North Way round the corner from our house. I think Tommy was the only kid I knew whose father wasn't Jewish, which was so unusual people used to say 'You do know Tommy's not Jewish?' all the time. They said it so often it almost became a catchphrase.

When I was 16, we left Hendon and moved to Regent's Park after the company had started to do well. The change in our financial status, combined with the change of address, meant I suddenly had a whole new group of friends, and I barely saw the Hendon and Golders Green crowd again. One day I was at a party near our new house, when a very flamboyant and confident boy came in wearing a college scarf. His name was Michael Green, and a couple of years later, Michael turned up at a party with another friend called Charles Saatchi. Michael and Charles would become important figures in my career, and Michael remains my best friend to this day. If I'm honest (much as I hate to admit it) our friendship – or more accurately the rivalry inherent in our friendship – was a big motivator in my career. In the years that followed, the three of us would push each other to succeed, and all three of our companies – Saatchi & Saatchi, Carlton Communications, and Ratners – benefited from our need to brag to one another when we met up for a game of snooker.

I've since heard several business commentators refer to our 'North London mafia', which was clearly a euphemism for being Jewish. My relationship with my faith has changed over the years, but as a kid I saw it as something social. I tried to observe the fast on Yom Kippur, but I think I only lasted until lunch time. Trying not to eat for a day was more of a game for me, a bet I could have with my friends. I couldn't stand sitting in the synagogue all day, as you're supposed to, and so I and my friends used to walk from one synagogue to the next synagogue just to see who was at those synagogues, a bit like a pub crawl.

My parents weren't particularly religious, in fact they then became Reform so they could sit together in the synagogue rather than my mother having to sit upstairs, and they certainly didn't go every week, only for the major feasts. If I'd had my way, I don't suppose I'd have gone at all, but my parents thought there was something odd about a Jew who didn't go to synagogue on Yom Kippur. I suspect they were only really worried about what the neighbours would think if I didn't go. The Fifties and Sixties was a God-fearing time for the Jews after the Holocaust, and most of my friends' parents wouldn't dream of not going to synagogue on important occasions, and some of them made sure they went every Saturday. My grandfather was unbelievably religious, and I wouldn't dare let him know that on a Saturday I might have gone on a bus.

In time, my parents became less observant, but their obsession with what the neighbours thought in those days was, I believe, the cause of a tragedy that scarred our family for ever. When I was 19, my sister Juliet met a boy called Barry who worked in a fish and chip shop, and even though it was his parents' shop, my parents didn't think it was a good enough occupation for a potential son-in-law. So my dad gave him a job as a manager of one of our shops, but there was a bigger problem: Barry wasn't Jewish.

My parents were convinced any marriage would be wrong and they told Barry he could only marry their daughter if he converted to Judaism. 'Marrying out' still had a huge social stigma attached to it, and despite the disapproval my grandparents had shown them when they'd got married, my parents still worried about what the neighbours might say. So Barry took lessons with a rabbi and began the conversion process. He even got circumcised in his twenties, so there can be no doubt that he was serious about my sister.

At this time, I was with my first serious girlfriend called Jackie, and I wanted to impress her by driving Barry's MGB. I pestered him for weeks, and he eventually relented. Cheekily, I assumed that because he'd given me permission once, that meant I could drive it any time I wanted. So whenever he called on Juliet, I took his car out for a drive, pulling up outside my friends' houses and showing off. Needless to say, I thought Barry was a great guy and I was thrilled he was going to be my brother-in-law. It came as a complete shock when, several months later, the rabbi refused him permission to convert.

Barry had had enough of the demands my parents had put on him, and the rabbi's rejection was the final straw. Although he said he still loved Juliet, he couldn't take the interference any more and so he broke off their engagement. This created hostility between my parents and my sister, which caused Juliet to slump into a serious depression. As the weeks went by she got worse and worse, and was eventually put on medication. It was an uncomfortable time to be at home, so I was glad when my new girlfriend's father invited me to stay with them at their apartment in Monte Carlo. Angela Trupp had previously been dating David Green, the brother of my best friend Michael, and our getting together had caused a bit of a rift between me and the Green brothers. At the time I didn't care: I knew I was more serious about Angela than I had been about Jackie because I would rather spend my Saturday afternoons with her than watching Arsenal at Highbury.

On that trip to Monte Carlo it was separate bedrooms, of course, but it nevertheless felt incredibly grown up going on holiday with my girlfriend. Angela's father was a successful businessman, and staying in the apartment in Monte Carlo was a real taste of the good life. However, a few days into the trip, Angela came to my room at 8 o'clock in the morning and told me she had some bad news.

'It's your sister', she said, 'she's taken an overdose'.

I didn't want to hear what she was going say next.

'And she's dead.'

My head suddenly rushed with emotions. My first thoughts were that I needed to get home, but those practical notions were swimming around with a volatile mix of grief and guilt, because I felt I had been such a rotten brother. I fluctuated between sensible and dramatic for a few hours as Angela and her family sorted out a flight back to London. I sat there having breakfast and was consumed by misery. I had never known anything like it.

The practicalities of leaving for the airport, the processes of check-ing in and boarding a plane helped to calm me down a bit, and Angela came with me for support. A few hours later, I was back in Regent's Park and as I turned my key in the lock, the door opened. It was my father. He gave me a big hug and said something crass like 'It's good to see you. There aren't many of you left.' To be fair, none of us knew what to say, and my mother was so grief-stricken that she didn't speak at all. She had been the one who'd found Juliet's body, and I think this traumatised her in ways the rest of us could only imagine. Certainly the one thing none of us said was 'It's your fault', but I don't think any of us were in any doubt that the way my parents had treated Juliet's relationship with Barry had contributed to her actions.

Denise, Diane, I and my parents barely left the house for the next four days as neighbours, friends, and relatives came to pay their respects. One person who didn't come to see us was Barry. He had severed all ties with the family after he broke off the engagement, but I heard through friends that he was completely devastated.

Many of the shop managers came to mourn as well – all of us had been in and out of the shops our whole lives and many of them had known Juliet since she was a toddler – and when my father's conversation inevitably turned to 'So, how's business then?' I made my excuses and left. I realised then just how seriously his operation several years before had affected him. He really didn't feel any pain. He could see that my mother was upset, but it was clear he didn't completely understand why. His daughter had died, killed herself even, and he just didn't show any emotion. A bomb could have gone off in the garden and he wouldn't have flinched. We all remembered the man he had been before the operation, a man of empathy and spirit, and seeing him like that at such a terrible time for the family only reminded us of the man we had lost.

My mother was too upset to go to the funeral, and the months that followed were incredibly tough. It was almost as if Juliet came between us as we each dealt with her death in private as best we could, and the family unravelled around her memory. It's terribly sad that that's how we dealt with it, and I had to force myself to remember the good times we'd had as a family, and what a fabulous sister she had been.

I was helped through my grief because a friend of mine who lived round the corner had lost his sister in exactly the same way the year before. I'd written him a letter at the time, which was very unusual for me because I wasn't very good at writing letters, and when Juliet died, he wrote to me. It helped me come to terms with the fact that death, even suicide, is just part of life. I know some people would look on my family as dysfunctional, but I think that every family has its fault lines and secrets.

In the days after Juliet's death I'd watch TV and see those adverts for washing powder with a family where everybody was healthy, happy, and smiling – the idealised caricature everyone supposedly aspires to – and it just seemed so fake. In real life people do die, people get ill, and people do not fit into perfect slots. So I still look back at my family as a normal family, even though one died, my father was ill, my mother was a bit eccentric, and I came bottom at school. I think that was pretty normal.

My mother's grief was without limits, although the coroner's conclusion that Juliet's had been an 'accidental death' was some comfort. Without wishing to be too graphic, she had choked on her own vomit, and this allowed my mother to believe that Juliet hadn't meant to kill herself. It wasn't much consolation, of course, and it was almost as if my mother was grieving on behalf of my father too. In the months afterwards, it became gradually clear that the trauma had affected her health. The list of medical complaints was a long one, and eventually, a few years later, she was diagnosed with cancer. In a way it was like she had willed her guilt to make her pay, but on the other hand she was adamant she was not going to succumb to the disease. In the years to come she would fight the cancer successfully, but it would come back somewhere else. At times, I'm ashamed to say, I became immune to what seemed like 'the next medical emergency'. Perhaps I was reacting with the thoughtlessness of youth, but maybe it was also a kind of survival mechanism because I just couldn't face the reality of losing my mother as well as my sister.

However, she continued to defy the doctors' prognoses for the next 30 years. Those decades were overshadowed by her constant battles with illness, and my parents would spend many, many months and a considerable amount of money chasing cures.

Juliet's death had another consequence, one that changed my life quite profoundly. Well aware that their meddling had been the cause of their daughter's heartbreak, my parents were determined that they would not make the same mistake with me. When I returned from Monte Carlo, my mother said something that I thought was a bit strange at the time:

'You can't go and stay with someone's family and not show that you're serious.'

I didn't pay it too much attention, but a few months later my parents went out and bought an engagement ring from friends of ours who ran a jewellers called Kutchinsky's. It was an awful ring, and we could have got it much cheaper from one of our wholesalers, but maybe they couldn't wait. It turned out they couldn't even wait for me to propose, and gave it to Angela themselves! I was 20, and even though Angela was a little older at 24, neither of us was ready for marriage. However, as we both came from the sort of families where you did what your parents told you to, we were married in February 1971 and moved into a house in Primrose Hill that Angela's father had bought for her.

CHAPTER 4

The Family Business

My father had trained to be a doctor before the war, but he found business far more challenging and exciting. He was an intelligent man and he told me that he thought business was a way of using all of your skills and knowledge, of using everything you had. He saw it as pitting his wits and brains against other men, like a game of chess, and felt it was the ultimate test of strategy and competition. Very early on, I assume he wanted to outperform his brothers and father who were all in the same trade. He used to read this book called *Strategy of Desire* that was based on always doing the opposite of what everybody else does. He found strategy fascinating, which meant he got a huge thrill out of being in business and that made him ambitious for success – there was little chance that he was going to stop at just the one shop in Richmond.

Although jewellery wasn't the most exciting sector to be in, my father reasoned there was very little competition and you could make a good profit margin on each transaction. There were a lot of independent companies in jewellery, as well as a few established firms like H. Samuel – and that meant he felt there was room for his business to grow.

His second shop was in Slough, and I remember being at home with my mother when I was very young and her being restless. She clearly thought she was missing out on something.

'Do you want to go and visit your father in his new shop?'

It was just about the most exciting thing I'd ever heard.

So we got on the Green Line bus from Hendon and spent most of the day getting there and back, but there was nothing else either of us would have rather done with our time. My mother was so in love with my father that she hated to be apart from him. They were like Siamese twins they were together so much, and when we turned up he was absolutely delighted.

The Slough shop was very profitable, and so my father quickly used his spare cashflow to open up a third branch in Hounslow. I can still remember the order in which all the shops opened, even though it's now 15 years since I left the company, and over 50 years since some of the branches started trading. After Hounslow came Clapham and Bedford. The first Oxford Street branch was Oxford Street 12, and then it was Luton 13, Watford 15, Colchester 23. It won't mean much to anyone else, but it reminds me just how much I loved the family business, down to the tiniest detail.

In those days, jewellery was really quite a respectable trade – our shops were all chandeliers and plush carpets, trying to look like a private bank – and it was seen as quite an achievement to be the manager of such a shop. Our managers all dressed in three-piece suits (they were all men in those days, of course) and kept eyeglasses in their pockets. It all looked very smart, and because it was important to appear above board, most jewellery shops were named after their owners – calling yourself Whistles or Oasis would have been too frivolous, so my father's shops all bore the family name, even though he later said that if he'd known there would eventually be so many shops he would have used a different name. For some reason, he didn't think Ratner was a good enough name to go above the door.

By the time I was eight or nine, my father had opened up six branches, and some of my happiest memories are of driving round in his second-hand Humber Supersnipe and visiting all the shops in one day. The fact that he was expanding meant it was a pretty hand-to-mouth existence, especially in March and April, which is still a deathly time for the jewellery business. It's all about Christmas in jewellery, so the family had money around January to pay the bills, but the rest of the year was always a bit tight. Each shop was leasehold – there was never any question of there being enough money to buy the freeholds – and the stock was bought on a sale-or-return basis in an attempt to keep profit margins wide enough to support the next phase of expansion.

My father was a great retailer, I can't over-emphasise that, and he was smart enough to work out how to do things more efficiently than his competitors. One of his great innovations was sending photos to each of the managers showing exactly how to lay out the shop window. One photograph would be of a pad of rings, another would be a display of watches, another would be the earrings display, and so every single shop was identical – including the signage above the door that never changed in the whole of Ratners' existence. Importantly, my father's photograph system meant that when a ring was sold it couldn't be replaced by any other ring, it had to be replaced by the ring in the photograph. That way he could easily ascertain what the bestsellers were and make sure that they were reordered. My father always said that we made 80% of our money from 20% of our lines, so identifying the bestsellers was crucial, and it remains the biggest lesson of my retail career. Many of the changes I would make in the future would be about ensuring our bestsellers were always in stock. So many retailers know this now that it's easy to overlook how innovative this was. I think one of the key successes of Argos, for example, is that they have this discipline whereby their catalogue is changed twice a year to eliminate the lines that don't sell. If you can exploit the best lines, you can make more profit, and a lot of retailers tend to replace things with what is available, not with what sells. My father also had the idea that every ring in a pad should be the same price, so customers could easily compare price ranges. It also meant that our windows weren't littered with tiny little price tags, and that meant our displays were very inviting.

My father observed his customers closely and learnt all he could from them. We were selling diamond rings for £25 in an era when the average take home pay was around £80 a month, so obviously people took a long time to make up their mind. In some cases they would come back month after month while they were saving up, or summoning the nerve to propose, and so my father realised how important it was that the window display stayed the same. If people came back and couldn't find what they wanted, they were unlikely to ask for it and he would lose the sale.

The window is the most important part of a jewellery shop, and this is something my Uncle Jack understood better than anyone else. After the merger between my father, my uncles, and my grandfather – a merger that meant, over the years, they would each claim to have founded the company – Jack's main role was finding new premises.

Jewellers need a lot of frontage so there's always something to catch the public's eye, but because the stock is made up of small items, the shops themselves can be pretty small inside. My Uncle Jack was a whiz at property and found us some very clever sites. In other kinds of shops, customers come in to browse, but in jewellery, the browsing is all done outside. This meant we could operate in a shop that was perhaps only 600 square feet, which meant there wasn't too much competition for them and Jack could usually negotiate quite hard on the price. Slough, which for years was our most profitable shop, was all frontage and so tiny inside that at Christmas there were queues out the door because you couldn't get more than a handful of people in the shop.

One way to get more frontage was to create an arcade where you have two L-shaped windows either side of a walkway entrance up to the shop's door. Another was to go for corner shops that had often been chopped about inside but still had frontage on two sides. Jack would only go for prime locations, and in those days it was very simple to tell if you were in the right place: if you were between Marks & Spencer and Woolworth's, you couldn't fail. There was a little stretch in every high street, more or less in the middle, where – as long as you were on the right side of the road – a jeweller's shop was pretty much guaranteed to thrive. We had our rules about location, and Jack would never take a shop in a secondary location, ever. This meant we had some fantastic corner locations. I remember Doncaster 27 was at the corner of two main shopping streets and it did phenomenally well, just by virtue of its location.

Jack ran the property side of the business practically single-handed. You didn't have a whole team of people as you would today, it was just him. Jack was a very understated man, but he was very effective and very methodical. He had a GOAD plan of every town centre in Britain that showed the layout of the town centres along with their occupiers and their lines of business. He marked out a big circle in green ink round what he regarded as the prime location, and shaded in each shop within that circle that he wanted to target. He would then come to a meeting and present the board with a proposition for a shop that would be accompanied not only by the GOAD plan, but also by photographs that had been taken the previous Saturday at 3 o'clock, which showed how busy the location was. Sensibly, he sifted out the shops that didn't quite match our criteria and only showed my father the best options: he'd learnt that there could be arguments over borderline decisions. I suspect he and Mr Hussein had worked out exactly what shops they wanted before those board meetings.

Jack was a key part of Ratners' early success, but I never once heard him boast about his achievements. There was even a famous family story that my grandfather had found a load of trophies in a cupboard and asked Jack what they were for.

'Oh, I won them at sports day.'

He'd won practically every race, but he'd never said anything to anyone. He was a very quiet fellow, which was probably a sensible approach when you were in business with my father and grandfather. The arguments between them were frequent and bitter. They hadn't got along for years before they went into business together, and to this day I'm not quite sure why they joined forces, especially as the old resentments never went away. My father often told the story of the day my grandfather visited his shop and lost his temper so badly that my grandfather took the one pad of diamond rings that my father had out of the window, threw them on the floor, and jumped on them. He had the most appalling, volatile temper, once he even picked up a plate of food and pushed it into my uncle's face! I can remember clearly several Sunday afternoons when my grandfather would drive from St Albans to Hendon for his lunch but would then leave after three minutes and drive all the way back because of some argument or other. And this was *before* my father's operation. There were endless squabbles, and the occasional bit of buck-passing, and in the end they all had to use different coloured pens – Jack was green, Leslie was blue, and David used red – so they would know who had authorised what! It makes you wonder why they ever merged their companies.

In the Fifties and Sixties, the sector was dominated by the Edgar family, who owned the H. Samuel chain. Their shops were four times the size of ours, and were beautifully fitted out. I always thought their shops were too big, and that they were just filling space by stocking gifts like cut glass decanters that I thought were a bit cheap. (Many years later, of course, when I made the speech that changed my life, I would have plenty of time to reflect on my reservations about the quality of H. Samuel's gifts.). H. Samuel was a publicly owned company, and they always had the very best locations.

For a long time, the second biggest name on the high street had been James Walker, but their policy had been not to open up branches wherever there was an H. Samuel. Of course, this made them a very attractive takeover prospect for H. Samuel, and when the two of them merged, Ratners seemed like a flea next to an elephant. H. Samuel also had a policy of owning the freehold of their shops, so they were an incredibly well-funded operation. They'd had 350 shops before the merger, and when they added hundreds of new stores overnight, it was difficult to compete.

As well as lots of small family-run jewellers, our other major competitor was the Ernest Jones chain. Jones was a much more upmarket jeweller, with about 60 shops. They had beautiful displays and were more of what we called a 'county' jeweller, which was a byword for expensive. Nothing like Tiffany or Cartier, today, but for Britain in the Sixties they were sophisticated, stocking Rolex watches and such like. If you'd asked anyone in the trade at the beginning of the Sixties what the likelihood was of Ratners taking over H. Samuel and Ernest Jones, they wouldn't have been able to answer because they'd have been laughing so much. But of course, that's what happened. Eventually.

CHAPTER 5

Growing the Business

At the end of the Fifties, the entire UK jewellery industry was probably worth about £500 million and naturally, my father had it in his mind to get as big a slice of that particular pie as possible. He noticed that the sort of customers he was getting into his shops was changing. What was once seen as the province of the rich was becoming much more diverse. His customers were no longer just bank managers and solicitors, but clerks and secretaries too. If Ratners could find the right products for this clientele, he realised he could open up a whole new market. It was around about then that he made the single smartest move of his career: he promoted a man called Terry Jordan.

After my father and Jack, Terry was the single most important person who worked at Ratners in the early days. He was our buyer, and getting the right buyer can make or break a jewellery business. In Terry, my father had the best in the country. Terry started off buying our costume jewellery, but it was clear he had real talent, and within a few months he took over the whole of our range.

Terry was a very personable guy, and he had what I can only call the 'common touch'. Even when Ratners became quite a big company, Terry still went to Butlin's for his holidays. He completely understood our customers and he knew absolutely what they wanted. He searched for merchandise that put us on a slightly lower rung than the more upmarket Samuel's and Walker's, and sure enough, the customers soon noticed. Not that there was any promotional stuff done in those days – no discounts, no sales, no gimmicks – it was all done on price. Our merchandise looked the business: our diamonds might have been a bit smaller, and our gold a bit lighter than something in Samuel's window, but to most people the only difference was the price. Our business really started to take off, but with the profits split between the four directors, I can't say I noticed the difference at home.

Terry's knack was to spot the jewellery that other buyers had overlooked. One of our big sellers was something called the Illusion ring. It had a tiny one-point diamond set in a big circle of white gold. Diamond cutting had just been refined, and the white gold was cut into lots of tiny facets so that from a distance it made the diamond look bigger. Nowadays people just buy a big diamond on their credit card, but our customers couldn't afford it then, and a lot of what Terry Jordan bought for us was jewellery that people could afford. It wasn't as cheap as the stuff that I became famous for selling 30 years later, but it was an awful lot cheaper than Samuel's and Walker's.

A big percentage of our sales came from watches. Most watches today are quartz, which is far more accurate than the old movement watches. That is a shame, because some of them were real works of craftsmanship, and our stock back then included some real collectors' pieces. We knew the Loftus family who ran Accurist – they had offices in Baker Street, not far from our head office on Oxford Street – and we got some great watches from them. Over the years, Ratners developed good relationships with all our suppliers, from Pollards who supplied the ring pads, to Manshaws the gold merchants, to the gem dealers in Hatton Garden. It was quite a small world, and as the business grew, we started to become quite well known. The jewellery trade was a tight-knit industry, and businesses thrived on the basis of individual relationships.

There was one other member of the team I really should talk about before I move on, and that's Massarat Hussein, although he was known to everyone in the business as Mr Hussein. He joined the company very early on as the accountant. These days he'd be called Financial

Director or Head of Finance, but back then it was just him and a pile of paperwork in a tiny room. You could barely see him behind his lever arch files and invoices. He worked so hard, frenetically, and did the work that a team of accountants would do these days. He wasn't paid all that well either, but he had so much respect for my father – he was a bit sycophantic towards him, if I'm honest – that he stayed with us for years, and years. He knew everyone in the company, and everyone knew him, and when my family refused to speak to each other, the role of messenger and peacemaker fell to him.

Ratners' head office was above our flagship Oxford Street branch. It also doubled as a store room, and there were boxes of merchandise on every available inch of floor space. It was a complete fire hazard, and if a fire officer had come he would have closed us down. There were boxes all the way up the stairs, but my father would not spend any money on warehouses or expensive offices. He used to say to the managers, 'Every penny that's spent, the customer has to see', and he went to ridiculous lengths to save money. Eventually there were so many boxes that we ran out of space, which meant a new member of staff didn't have an office. My father's solution?

'Build a shed on the fire escape!'

In the end there were about four men in that shed, and it was probably only their weight that stopped it blowing away in the wind.

It wasn't a coincidence that the shop below the offices was our best store, as the staff just had to pop upstairs to replace anything they'd sold out of. There were no computers in those days, and reordering stock for our other branches could take up to a week. My father used this as an excuse not to move or upgrade our offices, so much so that when it got really quite difficult to get up the stairs, he had this idea of designing a chute that would go down to the basement from the top floor. This was a real 'Heath Robinson' affair – he'd put the jewellery down the chute, and it would slide down to the basement where it was packed up and sent out to other shops. I can't have been the only one who thought that the whole thing was just going to collapse one day.

Another of my father's unusual decisions was cancelling our insurance. He reasoned that the chances of all 55 shops getting broken into on the same day were pretty slim. A couple might, he conceded, but not all of them, and we would be better off taking the hit than paying the premiums. It was an outrageous decision, but that was the way he was, and of course, it turned out to be a good one as we saved quite a lot of money.

Security is a big issue for the jewellery trade, and when alarms arrived on the scene it made sense for every shop to have one. We had a contract with Chubb Alarms to maintain the systems, but it was in the early days of the technology and they were pretty unreliable. They used to go off all the time and it drove us nuts. When my father got Chubb's bill, he decided to cancel the contract. So we had no alarms and no insurance – a ridiculous situation that no company would get itself into today. But my father, being my father, had his own solution: all our shops had security grills, and so he had signs made saying 'High voltage' and attached them to the shutters! His reckoning was that if there was a risk of getting electrocuted, no one would chance breaking in. This was long before dummy CCTV cameras and fake alarm units, and by and large my father's idea paid off. It saved us money, but in a sense it was unfortunate, because it gave my father the idea that all his outrageously daft ideas would pay off.

One such idea was the belief that no one bought jewellery in a shopping centre. In the early Sixties, we took a shop in the brand new Bullring in Birmingham, which was Britain's first American-style shopping mall. It seems crazy now, but it was considered extremely posh then and so we took a small unit in it. It was opened with a bit of a fanfare by the Duke of Edinburgh, and we all got very excited when he popped his head round the corner on the first day (the entire family had decamped to Birmingham for the occasion). But once we started trading there, the shop was a complete and utter disaster. It was behind the escalators in the basement, and no one knew we were there, but my father decided that that wasn't the problem: the problem, in his eyes, was that it was in a shopping centre at all.

The fact that other retailers there were taking huge profits wouldn't dissuade him.

After Birmingham, my father resolutely refused to ever open a shop in a shopping mall ever again. Brent Cross went by, Milton Keynes went by and by the end of the Sixties, we had lost out massively. Nevertheless, my father remained adamant that malls would never catch on. This was possibly his most disastrous decision, and in my opinion it was a major factor in Ratners making a loss in the early Eighties as we had forsaken the opportunity to lease the best premises in malls.

One day my father, in his peculiar wisdom, decided that he was not going to sell branded watches any more because the profit margin wasn't big enough. If Marks & Spencer could produce own-brand goods, then so could we. He had become obsessed with Marks & Spencer and wanted to learn from their success. Once we'd had the watches made, we needed a name for the brand, and I remember sitting round the dining table in our house in Hendon discussing what we were going to call it. In the end we came up with Accolade, but as soon as they hit the shelves we were sued by Accurist who accused us of passing them off. This is how naïve we were: none of us ever said 'let's have a name that sounds like Accurist', and none of us ever considered that we couldn't call our own brand of watch exactly what we wanted. Even though we had been very friendly with the Loftus family, they got annoyed with us and, to cut a long story short, they won the legal argument and we went back to the dining table to come up with another name. The second time round we came up with Caranade, which was an appalling name. Who would want a watch called Caranade on their wrist? Needless to say, they didn't sell well and Ratners lost a fair bit of money on the venture.

Another of my father's not-so-great ideas was our repair service. If we had sold you a faulty watch, we would come round to your house with a van, pick up your watch, repair it, and bring it back. I was still quite small and got very excited about this, because there would be a van with 'Ratners' on it and I thought that was fabulous! As a business idea, though, it absolutely stank and only came about because there was a woman three doors down who wanted her watch picked up. My uncles and grandfather knew it was a terrible idea, but my dad – as the managing director and biggest shareholder – bulldozed the idea through. Of course, once it was set up, the woman three doors down was the only person who phoned up for a repair.

The four of them – Leslie, Jack, David, and my grandfather – all sat in the office waiting for the phone to ring, and when it didn't, my grandfather went into my father's office and said, 'I told you it was a stupid idea, you don't listen to me for a second. You have these stupid ideas and you force them through and you never, ever learn.' He slammed the door and they started yelling at each other from their respective offices. They were hysterical, but the rest of the staff had come to see that as normal. Thankfully my father had built up so much goodwill with his staff – through the home purchase scheme, amongst other innovations – before his operation changed his personality, and because he had employed people of the calibre of Terry Jordan, the company was able to survive these occasional disasters.

CHAPTER 6

Going Public

By the early Sixties, Ratners was a pretty sizeable operation, but for a man with 30 or more shops bearing his name, my father didn't have a lot of money – he still took the bus to work. Profits had been reinvested and his earnings had always remained quite modest in proportion to his success. He resolved to change this by bringing in some private investment from a venture capital company.

ICFC, the Industrial and Commercial Finance Corporation, a forerunner to today's 3i, took a 20% stake in the company for £500,000 (which, if you account for inflation, probably isn't far off £7 million in today's money). Although my father was allowed to use some of that money to give himself a pay rise, it was a condition of the investment that the bulk of the cash had to be spent on expansion.

As anyone who watches *Dragons' Den* knows, investors put cash into businesses looking for a healthy return. And once the wealth has been generated, the investor will want to take their profits. So to get the cash, my father had promised two things: rapid expansion and a stock market flotation at the earliest possibility, something that would have a profound impact on the way the company operated.

He actually also promised a third thing to his investors: to remove my grandfather as the company chairman. It wasn't thought the City would look favourably on him as a chairman as I was told he had been declared bankrupt during the war. I never knew the circumstances, but bankruptcy was the kind of black mark institutional investors didn't like. Unsurprisingly, asking my grandfather to stand aside wasn't the easiest of negotiations, and he was very upset. However, as he stood to become quite wealthy from the eventual flotation, this helped him accept what was put to him as 'early retirement'. And when my grandfather left, David, the youngest brother – who was a very nice bloke and who had always been very close to my grandfather – took the decision to leave as well.

The ICFC investment was the kind of money that I certainly noticed at home, and of course, as nice cars started appearing in the drive-way and my parents started eating in London's best restaurants, this was a huge incentive for me to become knowledgeable in all aspects of business, not just serving customers on Saturday afternoons. I started to read the business pages for the first time, and began acquiring all sorts of useful bits of information about the wider world of finance and the mechanisms of investment. Not long afterwards, my father acknowledged my school career was never going to amount to anything and suggested I join the company full time.

On my first day of full-time work, I think I was just about as happy as a 15-year-old on £9 a week could be. I was sent to help out in the branch on the corner of Oxford Street and South Molton Street, and one of the main things I had to do was run up to the warehouse above our Marble Arch shop at the other end of Oxford Street whenever we ran out of stock, which was usually about every two hours. No one was on commission, but nevertheless everyone wanted to work for the best store – there was always a bit of rivalry between branches – and so stock had to be replaced quickly. Sometimes I ran so quickly I arrived back red-faced and out of breath. I was used as a gofer by everyone, and there weren't many days when I didn't find myself at the Red Star depot arranging for packages to be sent to our shops round the country.

The thing I liked most was serving customers, and I was a good salesman. When the customer came in, I really wanted to sell them something, and everything else in my career has stemmed from that desire. I was good enough to be promoted and was moved to the Wood Green branch as manager, where I'd previously been the Saturday boy. I couldn't have been much more than 17, and as it turned out, I was far too young for that kind of responsibility and was pretty useless at organising anything or keeping good enough records. I was quickly moved back to Oxford Street and given the title of Assistant Manager, although I still had to do what everyone told me to do.

Oxford Street, then as now, was the most exciting retail street in Britain. As soon as we opened our doors, customers would come in and there was never a chance to get bored. It sounds incredible now, but all the shops shut on Saturday afternoons. It was the busiest day of the retail week, and shops closed for half of it! What were we thinking? Needless to say, Sunday trading wasn't even in our vocabulary.

As the boss's son, there was no way I was going to get on in the business unless I got on with my workmates. Not only did I have to be seen to be working hard, but I had to show that I was keeping my job on merit, which meant chatting to customers and making the sales. I never had any airs and graces, and I used to go round to the bookmakers at lunchtime with the other members of staff and have a bet on the horses. It was important that they didn't look at me differently and that I was just an ordinary bloke working in the shop, just like everybody else.

Just to prove I wasn't getting any special treatment, I was put in charge of repairs, which was the worst job in the shop. With repairs, there are always arguments and even if you were apologetic it wasn't enough to appease the most disgruntled customers. At worst, it was argumentative, and at best it was repetitive – a large part of the job was just putting the faulty items in envelopes and writing out address labels. For me, the worst part of this was that I could see colleagues on the other side of the shop serving customers and making sales. I really hated dealing with the repairs.

However, learning about the jewellery trade from the bottom up would stand me in good stead for the future when I was running the company. Not only did I understand the business at every level, but

I also got to know our customers and our staff. Crucially, I was also able to earn the staff's respect and wasn't seen as an upstart. A few years after I joined the company, Mr Hussein got a bee in his bonnet about the calibre of our shop managers and persuaded my father that what Ratners needed was some university graduates. He hired six of them, and needless to say none of them lasted, because none of them had a work ethic and consequently they just didn't get respect from the staff. The fact that I'd been a dropout at school, a little ironically, actually really helped my career.

At this stage I had no financial stake in the company beyond my £9 a week income. I had no shares, and as far as I was concerned, no real chance of ever having them. My commitment to the company wasn't motivated by personal wealth, although obviously I would have benefited from my father's success, nor was I motivated by the thought that I would run the company. As a family business, there were plenty of reasons why it was far from a foregone conclusion that I would take over the reins. Aside from the family feuds of course, which could conceivably have led to the break-up of the company at any point, Jack might quite rightly have wanted to take over if my father ever left. And if Jack didn't want the job, his son Victor was another potential candidate. So, at this stage in my career I was in it for the sheer love of it, for being a part of the company that I had heard so much about at the dining table all my life.

In 1966, Ratners floated on the Stock Exchange and ICFC realised their investment. It was a landmark in the history of the business, and also of my family. 65% of the company was offered to the market, with my father and Jack retaining 15% and 12%, respectively. The rest was held by my grandfather and Uncle David. The flotation meant my father was very comfortably off, and not long afterwards we moved house to the very glamorous address of Park Village West in Regent's Park. I can imagine my mother loved telling the neighbours in Hendon what our forwarding address would be.

The cash raised on the stock market was to be used to grow the business and produce a return for our new shareholders. Although market regulations weren't as stringent then as they are now, it was still a big shift for my father and Jack. They had run their business exactly as they had chosen to for nearly two decades, and now they had interference from investors, regulators, and a newly installed non-executive director from the accountants Stoy Hayward called Alfred Davies. The biggest impact of the investment was that Ratners went from 50 shops in 1966, to 100 shops by the end of the decade.

It's hard to describe just how exciting that is. Being part of a growing business is a buzz for any employee, but when it's your family's business, and it's a business you love, every day was a thrill. My memories of the late Sixties – I was a bit too young for drugs and free love, so I remember more than most – are that every week was better than the last. Whether it was England winning the World Cup (an event I found too painful to watch and had to leave the house – it was only when I heard cheers from nearby houses that I realised we'd won), London producing the coolest music in the world, Carnaby Street becoming the centre of the fashion world, or seeing a Ratners shop spring up in pretty much every town in the country, I really felt like I was on a roll. In short, life was good.

My father decided to celebrate the flotation by taking the area managers out to lunch. Staff jollies these days are all limousines and air-conditioned coach trips, but my father had planned for us to get to the restaurant on the bus. People could never tell with my father whether he meant this to be a joke, or whether this was just him being disorganised, or mean, and they were too scared of him to ask. And because my mother was there, as always, no one even raised an eyebrow just in case she saw.

We piled on to the bus, and my father, being my father, got out a big cigar to smoke – it was a regular accessory to his camel hair coat and handmade gloves. Of course, the conductor approached him and said 'I'm sorry sir, but you can't smoke that on here' (you could only smoke on the top deck in those days). Well, we all stared silently, anticipating how my argumentative father would react.

He looked at the conductor, took another puff and announced: 'This cigar costs more than you earn in a week and I'm not putting it out'! It was so outrageous the conductor couldn't say anything but 'Yes, sir', and my father finished his cigar. I have no idea if he knew how funny he was, but even though he had become quite eccentric by then, he had this air of greatness about him. And because he never would give an inch, he actually got a lot of respect from the staff.

My father's behaviour was so erratic that people would often come to me with suggestions and concerns they didn't feel able to raise with him. Somehow, I remained his blue-eyed boy, and I could get away with saying things to him that no one else could. This had a couple of advantages – it meant I was very well informed about everything going on in the company, and when I put forward a good suggestion, my father always gave me the credit for it. Although it's not something I'm proud of now, back then I didn't correct him when he thought the good ideas were mine.

One of the complaints I often heard was that our diamond rings really weren't good enough. They were being made by our own factory in Camden Town, which was a subsidiary my father had called Jadales after Jack, David, and Leslie (our warehouse in Oxford Street was another subsidiary that my father named Mondales using the 'mon' from Montague, which is Jack's middle name).

Diamond rings are often bought by young couples, and young people tend to have incredibly good eyesight and can spot if gems are flawed or claws are crooked. It was therefore essential that our rings were produced with precision. When I told my father about the problems, I also offered to put things right by taking over the management of the factory.

'Give me a few months', I promised, 'and I'll get our ring sales back up to where they should be'.

Naturally, he took me up on my offer, and so at 19 I became responsible for a staff of 20 or so, contracts with suppliers worth tens of thousands of pounds, the accounts, premises, and precision machinery. Needless to say, I had bitten off more than I could chew, and although I was very effective at making changes and improving quality, I wasn't all that hot at keeping records.

I had been motivated to ask for the promotion and additional responsibilities because I was getting restless. I'd been working full time for four years by this stage, and felt it was time I had a job title that rewarded my commitment and hard work. If I'm honest, I was also looking around at some of my friends, and felt I was starting to be left behind.

I guess by then I would have been on a salary of around £5000 a year, which was substantial for a young man still living at home. But it wasn't as much as Michael Green was earning, and I knew this because at 19 he was already driving a Jaguar E-type. I was jealous, but I was also determined not to be left behind. Michael was making his money from a new venture he'd started after acquiring the rights to a machine that could personalise the names on direct mail. He'd rented plush offices in Brook Street, just a few minutes away from our shabby head office on Oxford Street. When I went to meet him for lunch, it was impossible not to see the difference in our status.

It was typical of Michael to behave like a millionaire long before he was one. As well as the Jag and luxury offices (he'd deliberately taken the ground floor so that you'd think the whole building was his!), he wore tailored suits and had bought a lovely mahogany desk that told visitors he saw himself as part of the establishment. It was all front, of course, but it convinced everyone around him that he was a serious operator. It certainly convinced him – his self-belief was incredible – and it had a huge effect on me too.

The impact of Michael's success was heightened by the fact that we hadn't spoken for six months. We had fallen out because I had started dating Angela, who had previously been going out with David, Michael's brother and business partner. As far as they were concerned I had somehow 'stolen' Angela and they had presented a united front of anger towards me. I hadn't been the only one after Angela – practically every boy in North London had had a crush on her – and I don't think they could quite believe she had ditched David for me. However, our friendship was too strong for that to come between us for long.

The Green brothers' change in fortunes made me wonder if I might have greater success if I struck out on my own too, but I guess when it came down to it I didn't really have the guts to do that, nor did I have the money to set myself up. I think I was a bit too comfortable and felt that I could achieve what I wanted to achieve – and maybe even had a better chance of achieving it – if I stayed with Ratners. It was a calculated risk though, as I was getting impatient for the kind of success I could see my friends having.

I resolved to turn the factory around and started making changes to our procedures, management structure, and products, but nothing I did could change my opinion that the company would be better off without the factory. However, I knew I would have to be seen to have given it more time before I could tell my father my conclusion. I knew I was just biding my time, and felt out-of-the-loop stuck up in Camden. Sad as it sounds, the highlight of my day became having lunch with my parents.

I used to leave at 12.45 pm and drive into the West End. In those days I used to park right outside the office, which had its front door in Great Portland Street. The chances of getting a ticket were remote, so I just parked on a yellow line for a couple of hours. I'd walk into my father's office and, usually, Mr Hussein was sitting there going through things and I'd sit on his settee and join in for 10 minutes and discuss what was going on. In those 10 minutes I felt connected again to the business, but then my mother would arrive – it was a bit of a company joke that she was always around – and she would join my father and me for lunch. After that, we used to take a look at 373 Oxford Street and chat to the staff, and on the way back to the office we'd see what other jewellers were doing and if there was anything we could learn from them. By the end of the decade, Ratners had a third shop on Oxford Street – my father was nothing if not ambitious – and so lunch took a little longer. At about 3 o'clock, my father would go back to his office, and I would go, reluctantly, back to the factory. I really felt like I was serving a sentence at that factory, and there were many, many times when I regretted volunteering to sort it out. I felt I would be there for ever, and after any row with my father, I would often think again about setting up on my own.

The company was not in the best shape, and it felt like our problems got suddenly worse when the stock market announced that H. Samuel had bought 20% of Ratners' stock. Suddenly our biggest rival owned a large piece of us, and we didn't know if it was a prelude to a takeover. Certainly our share price wasn't performing all that well, and Samuel's might be sizing up an opportunity. I couldn't shake the feeling that Samuel's interest in us was bad news: how could it be good for us to have a rival owning a piece of us?

I started to feel it was increasingly important for me to have a role at head office. I knew if I waited for my father or uncle to offer me a job, then I could be waiting a very long time. I had learnt at an early age that if you start asking people permission to do something, they'll say no. The answer is to just do it – if you start having meetings or discussions about it, you will never get it done. The problem was that there wasn't really a job available for me at head office, so I would have to find a way of making myself useful, and then indispensable.

I began to spend as little time at the factory as I could get away with and found any number of excuses to be at the office. However, it was so small, and so full of boxes, that there really wasn't any room for me. If anyone was away visiting shops or suppliers, then I would sit at their desk, or I would sit in with Mr Hussein and help out with the figures. I quickly realised that if I was going to be a part of the company, then I would need an office of my own. I managed to find somewhere else to store some boxes and created an office for myself in a tiny little room. Nevertheless, it was the turning point – all I had to do now was find some legitimate work to do.

Without a job title or a role, it wasn't going to be straightforward, especially as I had to be careful not to tread on anybody's – Terry's, Jack's, or my father's – toes. I used my ingenuity, and found myself

doing completely different things from day to day. For instance, we
had a problem when Jack wanted to take a lease on a shop in Belfast,
but we had reservations because of the Troubles. To make a decision,
we needed to know how well the competition was doing.

So I went into my office, picked up the phone and called H. Samuel
in Belfast.

'This is Head Office', I said, 'there seems to be a mistake on your
figures'.

'Really, I don't know how that could have happened.'

'Well we've got a figure of £13,600 for last week's takings.'

'Let me just check, Sir, but I think it was more than that.'

They went away and got me the correct figure. I was worried
about telling the board how I'd got the figures, because they were a
bit conservative, but I hadn't lied exactly: I really was calling from
head office, it was just the Ratners' head office and not H. Samuel's! It
worked so well that I started to call lots of rivals and got their figures
in the exact same way, and the information I learnt proved very useful
as we were pushed by the City to produce higher and higher profits
for our shareholders.

I proved so useful to the company that, at the age of 21, my father
asked me to join the board. It was just what I wanted to hear: it meant
he trusted me and valued my input. It also meant the other board members agreed to my promotion, and that was incredibly satisfying.

Not only did this mean a pay rise, which as a newlywed came in
very handy, it also meant I'd climbed the status ladder a bit. By then
I was also friends with Charles Saatchi who, like Michael Green, was
running a successful business with his brother and was well on his
way to his first million. Hanging out with Charles and Michael had
occasionally made me feel like a bit of a failure, but being a director of
a publicly limited company at 21 equalled their achievements.

The three of us would talk about the City, property prices, policy,
politicians, and tax law. We discussed problems we were facing with
our own companies, and we helped each other come up with solutions.
Although we were friends, we were also rivals, and we always wanted

to top each other's achievements. Charles was getting some very big clients at his advertising agency, Saatchi & Saatchi, and Michael was diversifying into other areas of marketing and media, and I sometimes felt like the little kid whose successes weren't a patch on those of his friends. I'm sure our need to brag to one another forced each of us to read more about our industries, and to learn more about high finance and City institutions than we might otherwise have done. None of us had been to university, but we spurred each other to get an education that was almost certainly more use to us than a degree.

Michael introduced me to his tailor and I spent ridiculous amounts of money on suits, and I guess I started to get a bit flash. A decade before power-dressing became fashionable in the Eighties, Michael and I were never out of sharp suits from Huntsman and Savile Row. The suits cost £1000 (I was only earning £10–15,000 a year at that time), but if Michael had a Huntsman suit then, of course, I had to have one too. What's even more ridiculous is that I have still got them in my loft, just in case I can ever fit into them again! At those prices, you don't throw them away. They were very old-fashioned, even for those days, and although I was still only in my early twenties, those suits made me feel like part of the establishment. I saw myself as 'respectable' because I was responsible for vast amounts of money, and I took that responsibility very seriously.

A generation on, I look at my children and their friends planning gap years and spending four years at university on a course that probably won't teach them all that much, and I do wonder if I missed out on something. Should I have gone travelling? Should I have taken the hint from Simon and Garfunkel and got a Greyhound bus across America? I certainly didn't want that then. As far as I saw it, I had exactly what I'd been brought up to expect – a directorship in the family firm, a wife, no doubt children were soon to follow, and if I hadn't felt so far behind my friends, I might have thought I'd made it.

Of course my material possessions weren't enough though. I was incredibly ambitious and I thought the more money I had the more satisfied I would become. I remember Michael's mother overhearing our conversation one Friday night and telling us there was more to life than money and profit. 'You should be going to Richmond Park or a gallery or the opera. Just take the dog out for a walk at least.' She really tried to persuade us that we were focusing on the wrong things. She was right, in a way, because there is much more to life than business. But at 21 it was all I was interested in – making money and everything that came with it. I lived for work, and I lived and breathed the jewellery business. I was desperate to make Ratners a household name.

CHAPTER 7

The Home Front

At different times in my life, I've been completely obsessed with utterly different things; and whether that's Arsenal football club, or collecting art or cycling, I have the kind of personality where I become consumed by my obsessions. For a large part of my career, my obsession was the business. I found every aspect of it fascinating, and by comparison, life at home seemed very humdrum. I think it's probably fair to say that I never fully engaged at home and left most of the household decisions to Angela. I can't tell now if the marriage suffered because I was obsessed with work, or if work took over my imagination because my marriage was – in some ways – an ephemeral part of my life. I know other friends in business who said they couldn't have made it without the support of their partner; I wonder if I became successful because my home life provided so few distractions.

Our marriage hadn't got off to the best start. We'd gone on honeymoon to the Bahamas on a package deal, which meant you couldn't change anything, and we were stuck with what the tour company had arranged. I don't really like being told what to do, so that didn't bode well, and then Angela got sun stroke, and after that I got food poisoning! While I was laid up, the hotel had arranged a party for all the honeymooners in the resort, and Angela went by herself. I didn't mind, but looking back that's how we operated – as two separate people who just happened to be married. When we came back from the honeymoon to the house in Primrose Hill, it seemed like real luxury and we were glad to be home.

My father-in-law had bought the house as a wedding present, and my parents had agreed to furnish it. The deal highlights just how sharp my father-in-law was – he had made an investment and the Ratners had shelled out on depreciating assets. We soon found out just what a bad investment the furniture had been when we returned from a trip to Monte Carlo to find that vandals had ruined everything in the house.

Two kids had broken in and trashed the place. They'd peed everywhere, they'd broken everything they could lay their hands on, they'd written on the walls, smashed the coffee table, and had completely torn our beautiful house to bits. My parents had gone round and tried to clear it up before we got back, which was very nice of them, but there was no hiding the damage. When the police came round, I asked them how the vandals had got in.

'They turned the handle.'

'Don't be daft. It can't be that easy.'

'You've got no locks on your doors.'

Looking back, I think that was a consequence of getting married at 21: we were both totally naive. How could we not have known that you needed to have a lock on the door? It was ridiculous, but then I never really paid attention to domestic matters. The perfect illustration of how disengaged I was from domesticity happened a year or so later: I was at home watching *Match of the Day* when a policeman walked into my bedroom.

'Good evening, sir.'

'What the hell are you doing here?'

'Didn't your wife tell you?'

'Tell me what?'

'You've been burgled sir.'

I was dumbstruck. Then I noticed that I was sitting in a room with drawers flung open and clothes strewn all over the place. A chair was upside down.

'Well', I said, 'I guess it is more of a mess than usual'.

In my defence, the house was usually a complete mess because we had two misbehaving beagles, and the damage Murphy and Kelly did to the house – they ate the lino, they ate the curtains – wasn't so very different from what the burglars had done. I think I loved those dogs precisely because they were naughty. One day I was sitting in a meeting with my father and some colleagues when one of the secretaries interrupted to tell me Angela was on the phone.

'Thank god you're there.'

'Why, what's up?'

'I was taking the dogs for a walk on Primrose Hill...'

'Yes.'

'And I don't know how it happened, but...'

'What's happened Angela?'

'I've lost Murphy.'

Well, that was the end of that meeting! I went straight home to help look for the dog. I eventually found him in Regent's Park and was so relieved I kissed him. I'd once spent nine hours wandering around the New Forest looking for him, and there wasn't much I wouldn't have done for those two dogs. Beagles have a reputation for being naughty, but Murphy was the naughtiest of the lot – he would jump up onto the settee and steal your dinner, and because we both loved the dogs so much they were never really told off. When we became parents, we agreed, we would have to learn the art of discipline in case our children turned out like Murphy and Kelly.

On the afternoon of March 30, 1974 two things happened. While Angela was in the delivery ward giving birth to our first child, Red Rum crossed the finish line first in the Grand National. I'd had £40 on him at 7–1 and pocketed £280. I had the feeling that our baby would be lucky despite the fact that she'd had a difficult birth. The labour seemed to go on for ever and although I knew Angela was doing the hard work, I was dealing with my parents who had insisted on being at the hospital. As the labour dragged on, my parents became convinced we'd got a bad doctor and started to make a huge fuss. I had a blazing row with them – I was embarrassed, furious, and nervous all at once – and eventually they left.

Suzanne was named after a Leonard Cohen song, and the moment I saw her, I became besotted with her. I absolutely loved being a father and although I admit to not being the best husband in the world in those days, no one could ever say I wasn't a very good father.

Our house wasn't much of a family home, so we decided to move somewhere more child-friendly. We found a house in Springfield Road in St John's Wood, which was a complete bargain at £47,500. Our house in Primrose Hill was worth about £32,000, and as I had no shares in Ratners or any assets of any kind to sell, it meant I would need to get a mortgage for the difference. The house had always been in Angela's name: her father had left my name off the deeds and had intimated to me that this was because he was quite sure Ratners would go bankrupt at some point and he didn't want his daughter's home to be at risk.

When my father-in-law found out about us getting a mortgage together, he sent me a letter – from his solicitor, no less – reminding me that the house was Angela's and that he didn't want me to have a stake in it. 'I've given it to Angela for her future and I don't want you to touch it.' I was reminded of the speech he'd given at our wedding reception, when he said that I would be treated as if I was his own son!

Angela went mad when I showed her the letter. She wanted to buy the house in Springfield Road as much as I did, and so she went to have a confrontation with her father. He wouldn't budge. And so Angela threatened him with goodness knows what, and he finally relented. It was one of the smartest financial moves of my life: in 1973, the market had just slumped and six months earlier the house in Springfield Road had been on the market for £125,000. We were in the middle of a deep recession and the stock market had dropped to 150 points. To put that in context, it's around 6000 points today. Things were so bad that the vendor had been forced to reduce the price to £75,000, but several buyers had been put off by surveyors' reports about subsidence. I thought the reports were rubbish – the whole street had subsidence and I couldn't see every house falling down – but nevertheless, he couldn't sell it to anyone but us and so we negotiated a spectacular price. Five years later the house was worth £500,000, but even if it hadn't proved so lucrative, I would still have great memories of that house as it's where our children grew up.

When she was two-and-a-half, Suzanne was presented with a baby sister, Lisa. I have to confess I don't remember a thing about Lisa's arrival: this was before it was popular for fathers to be present at births, and so I dropped Angela at the hospital and then went home and took a couple of sleeping pills. It was the only way I could cope with the anxiety. I was woken at 8 o'clock the following morning by the phone ringing. It was the doctor telling me that I had a second daughter. If I'm honest, I'd thought having a son would have been lovely, but after I laid eyes on Lisa, I never had that thought again.

When my girls were very tiny, I wanted to spend every spare minute with them. I forgot about Arsenal, I even switched off from work occasionally, and I just loved being at the house taking care of them and playing games. On Saturdays, I'd take them out with Michael and his two kids. We'd go to museums and ice rinks and anywhere else we could think to take them. I remember looking at friends of mine who weren't married, or who didn't have kids, and I was so desperately sorry for them because they didn't have what I had. Although my marriage was not a good marriage, I loved having a wife, children, a house, and family life. It felt permanent and secure, and I drew a lot of strength from that stability.

I suppose I was starting to see myself as quite an establishment figure and that's probably why I didn't think it was unusual for a 25-year-old to start collecting art. My father and I often went to Christies and the Mayfair art galleries on our way to or from lunch, and one day I saw a painting that captured my imagination so completely that I must have spent the best part of an hour looking at it. I like a painting with a story to it, and this was a street scene from the late 1800s of a man selling his wares to a passing customer. The detail in it was amazing and I wanted to buy it very badly, but it was £15,000, and that represented most of my annual salary. Instead of leaving the gallery with a purchase, I left with an obsession, and I started to learn everything I could about the artist who had made me think of something other than work for almost an hour. His name was John Atkinson Grimshaw, hardly a household name, but nevertheless one of the most collectable British landscape painters.

When I looked at his paintings, I felt myself transported back in time, beyond my childhood to Victorian times, but it wasn't like a book or a film, I really felt drawn into the scene. I wanted to understand how he had created such an atmosphere and, as is the way when I get obsessed about something, I began taking art appreciation classes in the evening. As art was something I was passionate about, I learnt easily and reached A-level standard without much effort.

One Saturday morning, long after Angela had got up and made breakfast for the girls, I stayed in bed reading. I was so engrossed that I hadn't heard the front door bell, and it was a bit of a shock when Michael walked in: apparently we had made an arrangement to go out.

'What's all this', he said, looking at the huge file on the bed. 'Still working?'

He picked the papers up, expecting spreadsheets and order books, and was pretty stunned to find biographical notes about Atkinson Grimshaw and essays on art history. He then told me that his wife took gallery tours with a guide on Tuesday afternoons, so I started to tag along to those, eventually taking a lecturer with me to the Leeds City Art Gallery where they had the biggest collection of Grimshaw's work. And while I was there, I toured the surrounding countryside and visited the places where he'd painted. I knew that when I had the money, I would buy whatever I could of his work.

It was becoming clear that I had expensive tastes – and if I was ever going to indulge them, I was going to have to earn some serious money. To be honest, in the mid-Seventies, there was no guarantee that any money would come from Ratners. My father's behaviour had started to alienate a few key members of staff, and although we were big enough by this stage to cope with a bit of staff turnover, it contributed to a period of stagnation. It was clear the City brokers would rather leave my troublesome father alone than apply pressure to get him to produce better returns – after all, who knew how he would react? We were too small to have been of interest to the financial pages or institutional investors, and so we were left to our own unspectacular devices for a few years, occasionally making progress, occasionally making mistakes.

One of our bigger mistakes in those days was our expansion into The Netherlands. Jack had been approached by a Dutch estate agent with an offer to take over some leases, and after much discussion we opened in Amsterdam, Rotterdam, and The Hague in 1977. Even though the shops lost money from the start, my father continued with his folly until we had six outlets in Holland. I think if we could have got out of the leases we would have walked away, but the financial penalty for terminating the contract early meant it made sense to stay put.

We tried to analyse why the shops were doing so badly – we had good sites, the jewellery had sold well in Britain so we knew it was fashionable, and the prices were competitive. We were really tearing our hair out trying to see how we could turn it around. An obvious thing to change was the management, so we removed the Dutch MD. What happened next is both hilarious and terrifying: while we were recruiting a new MD for the Dutch division, my father learnt that our tea lady was Dutch and appointed her to the position! I had been hearing stories for a few months from managers that my father was falling asleep in meetings, or that he had been found asleep in his office. I hadn't wanted to face the fact that my father was possibly no longer up to the job, but the appointment of the tea lady to MD of our overseas division was the moment I knew that he had, to be frank, lost the plot, and that it would be up to me to take control. He was only 60 years old, but it was clear that his health was deteriorating. It was painful to see such a brilliant man decline.

Still, the Dutch tea lady served her purpose: she was able to tell us why we were doing so badly in Holland. In the run up to Christmas we checked to make sure we'd got all the orders in, but she hadn't increased her stock for the December boom.

'Oh no', she said, 'we don't really exchange gifts at Christmas in Holland'.

That explained everything. With no Christmas boom, there really was no point in being in business there at all, and we took the decision to close the branches down and pay the penalty fee. At the time, I thought that would prove to be the worst mistake in Ratners' history. Little did I know.

CHAPTER 8

Downturn

The late Seventies was a very tough time for the company: not only was Holland draining our profits, but in several of our best towns, a new jewellery chain called Terry's was opening up right next to us. Not down the street or round the corner, but the very next shop. In their windows they had posters that said 'compare our prices with Ratners', so of course the customers did, and they shopped at Terry's. There was a bit of a company joke that the Terry behind the name was our own buyer, Terry Jordan, because the new chain had such good stock. We then heard some rumours from outside the company that Terry had a couple of his own shops, but we knew this was because his wife had a small chain of hairdressing salons.

Perhaps these rumours were more corrosive in my father's brain, and the rows between him and Terry increased both in number and intensity. My father had pushed several other loyal employees out of the company through his behaviour, and after one particularly pointless attack, Terry simply said 'I had enough of this in the army and I really don't need to be treated like this any more'. He resigned, which was a huge blow to the company, and we were all furious with my father for forcing our biggest asset out of the business. Without Terry, we all knew Ratners would suffer.

It was only once Terry had left us in 1978 that we found out the rumours about him were true – he really was the man behind our new rival. My father, understandably, was furious. For the last couple of years with us he had taken our salary but opened up shops in direct competition to us. My father thought his actions were nothing short of criminal, and called him every foul name he had ever heard. I was stunned and hurt too, but I could also understand why Terry had done it: he knew he was the reason behind our success, and in the years he had worked for us, he had seen my father become extremely wealthy while he was still on a salary. Terry knew that if he had the talent to make millions for Ratners, he could make millions for himself. While I was angry at his betrayal, there was a part of me that admired his decision. Of course, I never told my father this.

As new branches of Terry's continued opening up next door to our shops, and my father's acumen continued to falter, I took it upon myself to take more control of the business. I was a bit like a minister-without-portfolio in that I didn't really have a role or even a job title. This meant I found myself doing whatever needed to be done, but it also meant I had a licence to get involved with any aspect of the business that I thought needed my attention.

One of my priorities was finding a suitable replacement for Terry. We had employed a couple of buyers in quick succession who had bought expensive stock that didn't sell at all well, and I could never quite shake the suspicion that they were taking kickbacks from the suppliers. The buyer was such an important position for us, and I knew I needed someone in that role I could trust, so I asked my cousin Victor, Jack's son, to take over the buying side of the business. Victor was extremely bright – he had studied law at Leeds University – and had the benefit of having been around the jewellery trade all his life. While he didn't have Terry's magic touch, I thought he had pretty good instincts about the merchandise – he wanted to take us slightly upmarket – and he established good relationships with the suppliers.

I took it upon myself to bring in better watches, and started to negotiate deals that allowed us to compete with Terry's. I had a meeting with Seiko and asked them who their biggest customer was, and I was surprised to hear it was a relatively small chain called Green and Simons. They took all Seiko's end-of-line stock and were therefore able to sell it for 30–40% below the list price. I decided to do the same, only with brand new models, and our watch sales started to improve. Deals like that impressed the board, and it was great to be given the credit for the success.

In 1979, two things happened in my life that would prove very significant: firstly, I turned 30 and secondly, Margaret Thatcher was elected Prime Minister. When she won the election, her success was credited in part to the advertising campaign devised by Saatchi and Saatchi and the 'Labour isn't working' posters that had sprung up around Britain. Suddenly one of my best friends was not just being fêted by his peers and getting impressive profiles in the weekend papers, but more than that, Charles was also at the heart of government and had the ear of the most exciting politician the country had seen since Churchill.

It's not like there was some dramatic moment on my 30th birthday when I resolved to make more of myself, but over a period of months, I began to take stock and, in my opinion, I just didn't think I had achieved enough. I could sense that Mrs Thatcher was going to bring huge changes to business and to the country, and I realised that I wanted, very much, to play my part in those changes. I wanted not just to measure up to Charles and Michael, whose Carlton Communications was going from strength to strength, I also wanted to measure up to the opportunities that we all sensed the new decade would bring. I remember playing snooker with Michael and Charles – the three of us had started to play at my parent's place in Regent's Park, where there was a full-size table in the basement – and how fired up we all were about our immediate futures. I realised, however, that there was one major obstacle in my path – and that was my father.

I was in no doubt that I wanted the responsibilities and challenges of taking over Ratners. I wanted to turn the business around and get the share price back up: more than anything, I wanted to make the business a success again, but I felt so much loyalty to my father that I couldn't see how I could ask him to stand aside.

My Uncle Jack was, of course, another candidate to take over from my father, but he could see that the watch deals I was putting together were making up a big slice of our profits, and he proved surprisingly supportive of my ambitions. Mr Hussein also approved of promoting me, and so I put a suggestion to my father that he make me joint MD. Given that he was increasingly spending time away from the office trying to find cures for my mother's continuing battle with cancer in hospitals all over the world, he agreed without too much deliberation. I guessed he would rather that I took over than Jack, and so at our next board meeting my promotion was approved. At 30, I had become the managing director of a company with 130 stores nationwide, an annual turnover of £27 million and a staff of 500. If I hadn't been so hungry for greater success, I might have stopped to think I was doing quite well for myself.

My promotion had meant a pay rise and a bonus of my first shares in the company, around £20,000 worth. Over the years I used the company share option scheme to increase my holding to around 1% of the total stock. My salary was still fairly modest for a managing director – I was now earning around £26,000 – and so I looked around for other ways to increase my wealth. When my brother-in-law mentioned that the house opposite their place in Hampstead had come on the market substantially below value, I saw an opportunity to get some cash together.

I went to see the estate agent and agreed to buy it, because in those days you didn't need a cash deposit to get sale contracts drawn up. I then went to see another estate agent in St John's Wood and told him I had agreed to buy a house that I could no longer afford. When I told him where the house was and the price I had agreed for it, he said he would have no problem selling the contract on. For a fee of £1000 he found me a buyer, and one afternoon a couple of weeks later I drove to my solicitor's and signed the contract to buy the house, then drove to another solicitor's and signed over the contract to the new buyer. When I had done this, I was handed a cheque for £15,000.

I thought this was a terrific amount of money to have made in an afternoon, but I subsequently found out that the man I sold the contract to had sold it on himself, netting an identical amount of money. I could have kicked myself for selling myself short, but in the end I wasn't too bothered, as £15,000 was exactly the amount I needed to buy my first Atkinson Grimshaw painting. I had found it in the Richard Green gallery, and when I put it on the wall in my living room, it completely transformed the room. It was called Autumn Gold, and it was of a tree-lined road. I guess it was a bit chocolate-boxy, but it was absolutely stunning and I got an enormous thrill from owning it, from getting as close as I liked to brushwork and seeing it whenever I wanted to. Over the next few years, I bought several of his pieces, as well as a few paintings by Tissot and some minor French Impressionists.

In the early Eighties, Terry Jordan continued to open shops in competition with us. Eventually, he had 26 stores and in those 26 towns, our profits took a hammering. Our average turnover in those days was £500,000 a year per shop, but when we went up against Terry's, that figure slumped to £400,000. I was beginning to wonder how we had ever let Terry leave us.

We also had two badly performing shops in the North East, but Terry's shops were all in the South, so I couldn't work out why. I asked the managers of our Newcastle and Sunderland branches why they thought our figures were down, and without hesitation they both told me the name of a local jeweller, Robert Anthony. I got straight in the car and went to check out our new rival.

Robert Anthony had just the two shops, and I realised if he expanded then Ratners would suffer, so I wanted to find out what techniques he was using – and if we could steal them. I was surprised to find his shops were even brasher than Terry's, and it was clear why he was doing so well. Where Terry's would have a poster that said 'Compare our prices', Anthony's had posters that promised diamond rings for £60. It sounds bizarre now, but advertising how cheap you were was unheard of in the jewellery business: we didn't even have January sales in those days. Suddenly people who had never thought of buying jewellery before realised they could afford it: he had tapped into a whole new market.

I've always said that I'm not a great innovator, but I'm not slow at copying someone else's innovations. I could see that other jewellers were succeeding where we were failing, and I sensed that if we could learn from other people's successes, our massive high street presence meant we could have an incredibly profitable business.

I decided to replicate as many of Terry's and Robert Anthony's ideas as I could, and the first thing I did was put posters in our windows. Designing the posters became my job, and as a consequence I started to take responsibility for the whole of Ratners' marketing. The posters were really quite a shocking thing for an established jeweller to use – displays were meant to look respectable and expensive. Screaming to your customers that you had special offers and discounts was seen as highly inappropriate by a lot of operators.

Of course, the posters meant we had to have something to shout about, and as I realised we couldn't compete on jewellery, it would have to be on watches. Terry had made the decision not to sell watches as the margin on them wasn't as good as the margins he could make on jewellery. Not selling watches meant he didn't incur the costs involved in selling watches – the display space, the staff time, etc. – and that in turn meant he could reduce his margin on jewellery that little bit further and hurt Ratners even more in like-for-like comparisons. But as he didn't sell watches, it gave us a chance to steal back some of our old customers.

In the early Eighties, what would soon be labelled 'Thatcherism' was changing the high street. Young customers had money and were no longer impressed by the prestige of established brands. New manu-facturers like Swatch – who made plastic watches in a range of funky colours – and LED digital watches were changing the market. Suddenly it was very uncool not to have a digital watch, and customers who had perfectly lovely wind-up watches were looking to upgrade. I realised that if we got our watch strategy right, we could get a lot of customers through our doors and take the fight to Terry.

One of the benefits of being in the same trade for so long is that you get to know a lot of people and build up meaningful relationships with contacts and clients. One of the operators I'd always got on well with was the Beaverbrooks chain. I knew they were having success selling watches, so I went to meet with them. I respected them and was pretty sure I could learn from them. Their head office was in St Anne's, and the first thing I did when I got there was study their window display. They were selling a good range of the top brands and they had a poster that said 'Every watch sold below list price', which I thought was very intriguing. I wondered if the public knew that 'list price' meant the price set by the manufacturers, but it still seemed like a good offer. It was only on closer inspection that I realised their discounts on some of the watches were just a pound below the list price, but of course that didn't matter, as long as the poster got people through the front door.

Over lunch, one of the Beaverbrook family asked me 'what I was doing about Swatch'? I said I didn't really understand the question.

'They're insisting that we can't offer a discount. They say it cheapens the brand. We're going to have to remove the poster.'

I wasn't as gentlemanly as them, and as soon as I got back to the office, one of the very first things I did was call the printers and order posters for every shop that said 'Every watch below list price', and it was only in the small print that it said 'Except Swatch'. When the sales figures started to come in, it was clear my posters were making a difference, and it was small successes like that that enabled me to assert control over the company and gain the respect of Jack and my father.

I was determined to make Ratners the biggest jeweller's in the country, if not the world. I was hugely ambitious for the company, and for myself. I had recently seen Michael Green float Carlton on the stock market, and when we played snooker he would boast that his company was worth more than mine. Ratners had been in business nearly three times longer than Carlton, and it hurt to realise Michael's bragging was right: his market capitalisation – at £20 million – was greater than ours. Sometimes the pettiest of rivalries can be a great spur for future achievement, and Michael's success made me more determined than ever to turn Ratners around.

In the early Eighties, Charles, Michael, and I would sometimes play snooker five nights a week. We were all gunning for greater and greater success, and we used each other as sounding boards for options and strategies. Being married hadn't really changed my lifestyle all that much, and while nothing was wrong at home, I just preferred playing snooker with my friends and talking about business. The difference was that I went home to St John's Wood afterwards rather than to my old room upstairs.

Each week, I travelled to different parts of the country, turning up in shops unannounced to see how the branches were getting on. If there were new members of staff who didn't recognise me, I pretended to be a customer so I could see how well they served me. I spent quite a lot of time with the managers – I still loved being in our shops and observing how our customers made their decisions – and was trusted with information they might be too nervous of telling my father. I had known a few of them all my life, and walking into their shops was like walking into a friend's house. It was the part of the job I loved the most, and it became even more important that I had a strong working relationship with the managers when my father's behaviour towards our staff became increasingly aloof.

For instance, we had an area managers' meeting at our office. Many of them had been shop managers before, and in some cases they had been with the company for a decade or more. One of our longest-serving area managers was Mr Rockell, who looked after the South West. He and my father were talking about the merits of LED watches: although they sold by the bucket load, they were incredibly unreliable and we were getting hundreds sent in for repairs. Mr Rockell thought that perhaps we should stop stocking them.

'I've been in the jewellery business thirty years', my father said in a patronising way, 'and quite frankly you don't know what you're talking about. Mr Rockell, if I had to do without either the LED watches or you, it would be you.'

That's how rude my father had become, and so perhaps it's not so surprising that we found ourselves with quite a high staff turnover. My solution was to promote from within, and this proved to be very successful. An assistant manager from one branch was encouraged to apply for the vacant manager's position at the neighbouring branch, and this in turn created a chance for the counter staff in the first branch to become assistant manager. We gave staff opportunities they were not getting in other organisations, and this fostered loyalty and excitement among them. It meant we had some very young managers – a couple were only 20 – but they knew they'd been given a chance to prove themselves, and they worked hard to show my faith in them hadn't been misplaced.

Not all my ideas were good ones, however. In the run up to Christmas 1983, the sales forecast wasn't looking good. Not only was Terry's continuing to take market share, but earlier in the year the owners of Argos, British American Tobacco, had started selling Argos jewellery separately on the high street. Their Jewellers' Guild shops stocked very similar products to us, and it was clear they were targeting the same sort of customer. With a huge international company like BAT behind them, they had deep enough pockets to discount to such a level that they could really do us harm. I decided that the way to combat the combined threat from Terry's and the Jewellers' Guild was to advertise on television.

I went to an advertising agency and they came up with a Christmas campaign for us. I don't think I'd realised quite how expensive television advertising could be, but in the *Coronation Street* ad break, 30 seconds of air time cost tens of thousands of pounds. And as advertising only works if the public sees your ad often enough, I found myself committing to spending £100,000 on a method of promotion we'd never tried before.

At first I was very excited. When the VHS tape of our advert arrived, I took my video recorder from home into the office and invited all the area managers in to view it. The only place to put the TV was on the window ledge, and the only way the window ledge was wide enough was if I opened the window. So we all crammed into what was now my freezing cold office to watch 30 seconds of TV magic. The advert wasn't really any better than OK, but we were all fairly confident it would get Christmas shoppers through our door. Nothing had really changed since my father had opened his first shop – the jewellery trade was still about Christmas. If you failed at Christmas, you didn't have too many reasons to be hopeful for the new year.

Perhaps what happened next was a bit of an omen. My father was cold, and being single-minded, this was the only thing he could think about. As he marched up to the window and slammed it shut, it never occurred to him that closing the window would push my TV off the window sill... and onto the pavement below! Thankfully, no one was hurt.

Despite our optimism in that meeting, the TV campaign was an incredibly expensive disaster. Television just wasn't the medium for advertising jewellery shops, and a couple of decades on, I'm still a little surprised at just how well jewellery sells through shopping channels. We could have spent a lot less money putting adverts in newspapers and magazines and got much better results.

With Terry's and the Jewellers' Guild eating away at our profits and my father's behaviour becoming increasingly bizarre, it didn't seem to me that 1984 was going to be a good year. Sidney Simons, the head of one of the independent chains –Green and Simons – came into my office one day and he assessed our situation:

'H. Samuel own 20 per cent of you. British American Tobacco are one of the richest companies on the planet. Every week your sales are down. Your father's hardly ever here. You're not going to survive.'

I couldn't believe he'd said it, but I knew there was a chance he was right. A few weeks later, I walked into Mr Hussein's office, checking up on an invoice, and I was shocked to find him in tears.

'What's wrong?' I assumed it was his wife or some personal issue, but I could tell from the way he looked up at me that wasn't it. He suddenly looked 20 years older than the last time I'd seen him.

'I don't know what we can do', he said at last. 'We've got no money, the share price is down to 27p, we are going nowhere...' He tailed off. 'Your father thinks it will be all right, but it won't.'

I knew the share price had been slumping, but I hadn't realised it had *halved* in the past year. I became really quite terrified: I had children, a mortgage, a wife, and all of a sudden those things seemed in jeopardy. It almost felt as if my future was slipping away.

Whatever ground Ratners lost, it seemed to us that Terry Jordan gained it. We became obsessed with Terry – he was clearly making money, so we knew it wasn't that the jewellery business was in trouble, it was just *our* business. We heard that Terry was opening up in Southampton, and shortly afterwards my father announced he was going to pay a visit to our Southampton shop. I sensed there was an ulterior motive.

By this stage, my father was practically blind in one eye as a consequence of the operation to remove his tumour all those years before, but he nevertheless insisted on driving himself. My mother went with him, of course, and on the way down he crashed his Rolls Royce. I'm not sure what happened to the car, but they were taken the rest of the way by a lorry driver. When they got to Southampton, my father was so disorientated that he didn't realise the cab of the lorry was high up: he opened the door and fell several feet to the ground. I can only imagine the sorry state he must have been in when he finally arrived at our shop. My sick mother and my frail father stood outside Ratners and watched in horror as customer after customer walked past our shop and straight into Terry's next door.

When my parents returned from the Southampton trip, it was clear to me that my father was too shattered – physically and emotionally – to pick himself up and claw the business back from the brink.

'How was Terry Jordan?' I asked as nonchalantly as I could, as I stood in the door of my father's office.

'Oh, he was very busy. He'd just opened up so he was getting a lot of interest.'

The tone of my father's voice told me he was putting the best spin he possibly could on it. The truth was he felt Terry Jordan was stealing our customers, and stealing our business. It was painful to see my father so distraught, and the panic that the company was slipping through our fingers was gnawing away at me. This was the company I loved like it was part of my family – in many ways it *was* part of my family – and the sense of grief and anger was intense.

It was clear my father was not up for the fight and I realised that if the company was going to survive, it would be down to me to rescue it. I knew exactly what I needed to do to turn it around – I had actually known for some time – but I also knew that it was a move my father would never support. My loyalty to my father and my loyalty to the company was split, but I knew I would have to betray one to save the other. I picked up the phone and made an appointment that would change my life.

CHAPTER 9

Taking Over

If you had said to me at the beginning of 1984 that in two years' time I would be awarded Retailer of the Year, or that I would be having private lunches with Margaret Thatcher, or that Ratners would become the biggest jeweller in the country, I would have told you that you had a pretty cruel sense of humour. As I got in my car and drove through West London to Uxbridge, I had no idea that the deal I was about to strike would have such a profound impact on my life.

I had to check the A–Z a couple of times, but I eventually found the Italian restaurant I was looking for. As I parked the car I wasn't sure how much money to put in the meter: the meeting could be over in five minutes, or it could go on for hours. I decided to be optimistic and put in all the change I had. When I walked into the restaurant, Terry Jordan was already at the table.

It was actually quite nice to see him. I had known him since I was a child, and it was like seeing an old friend rather than a sworn enemy. There was plenty to catch up on, but of course, there was only one reason I was there.

'I'd like to buy your company.'

He smiled. 'That's funny, because I'd like to sell it to you. If you've got £4 million, that is.'

Terry had always been a very down-to-earth bloke, a real call-a-spade-a-spade kind of guy, and I knew when he said he wanted

£4 million that that was the price he would accept. Anyway, I was so pleased that I wasn't minded to bargain with him. If I was right, the deal would be worth a lot more to Ratners than we would be paying him.

I told him I could find the cash, there was just one condition to the deal: that he had to come back and work for us. At the time he was 50 and looking forward to an early retirement: he agreed to come back to Ratners until he was 55. As we talked, I suddenly felt the future coming into focus: with Terry back on board, anything seemed possible. Even finding the £4 million. Even persuading my father.

'Shall we shake on it?' I asked.

'There is just one more thing.'

'What is it?'

'I'm assuming that you're here because you're running the company now. As you know, your father and I fell out fairly badly. This is only going to work if I deal with you.'

I gave him my word that my father was now pretty much a back-room figure.

'I'm in charge', I lied, 'you'll always be dealing with me'.

When I got back to our offices, I didn't quite know where to start. Somehow I had to find £4 million, get my father's permission to bring Terry back, and then once I got that permission I would have to, effectively, fire my own father. I was nevertheless excited – buying a profitable chain of 26 shops for £4 million was an incredibly good price, but to Terry – who wasn't even taking that huge a salary – it was as much money as he could probably imagine. This was the guy who went to Butlin's for his holidays.

I had discussed my plan with Mr Hussein before I'd left to meet Terry, and once we knew what kind of money we had to raise, he set up meetings with the banks and brokers. My father had always used a firm of brokers called Grieveson Grant, and I wanted to bring in a fresh approach, so I called one of the biggest firms of City brokers, Morgan Grenfell. I spoke to a very impressive guy there called Roger Selig, who was one of their senior directors and advised me the best way to buy Terry's was to raise £2 million through a rights issue. In addition, we would give him a loan note for £1 million and a further £1 million in shares. However, there weren't too many investors eager to put their money into middle-ranking, underperforming retailers, so the shares would have to be issued at a very competitive price. When we had pieced the deal together, I showed the paperwork for the proposed takeover to my father. He was incredibly hurt that I could even suggest such a move.

'I wouldn't touch that crook's business with a barge pole', he snapped as he stormed out of his office. He still thought Terry had 'stolen' our customers and couldn't stand the thought that he might get his hands on some of our shares. Unbeknown to me, he got straight on the phone to Grieveson Grant and asked them to come up with an alternative option. My father knew the business was in trouble, and deep down he probably knew it was the right time for him to step down, but there was no way he would let Terry be our saviour.

A couple of days later Mr Hussein rushed into my office.

'Your father's got Grieveson Grant with him. They've found him an alternative deal.'

This was pretty chilling news. I knew my father could be bloody minded, and once he had made a decision it might be impossible to make him change his mind. I needed to do something quickly. I called Roger Selig but was told he was in a meeting. So I spoke to his assistant Crispin Wright, and when I told him what was happening, he leapt into action.

'I'll be there as soon as I can.'

Crispin's office was in the City, and with London traffic that meant he was probably a half-hour cab ride away from our offices in the West End, but he came bursting through my door in less than 12 minutes. He'd jumped on the Tube and run from the station.

'Not too late am I?'

When I walked into my father's office with a broker from Morgan Grenfell, everyone was surprised. The fact that I'd got such a high-calibre firm involved made them realise that buying Terry's wasn't just Gerald's silly pipe dream. If Morgan Grenfell were behind it, then it must be a serious deal. However, my father still wasn't interested.

Grieveson Grant had told him the Terry's deal was far too expensive and instead had brought him a deal that would lock Terry out. They had found a Scots jeweller who would pay my father and Jack £1 million in cash for their shares. This would signal their retirement, something I was pleased to see my father was considering, but it also meant that the Scot would have taken control of our company for just £1 million. At the time Ratners was worth around £13 million, and I thought it was a ridiculous, not to say insulting, deal.

Jack was called in to make a decision. He listened to both options and, to my great relief, he chose the Terry's deal. At that point Nick Redmain and Tom Wyatt from Grieveson Grant left, and my father — extremely reluctantly — agreed to buy Terry's.

Ratners had a contract with Grieveson Grant that meant they would be asked to handle the rights issue even though I wanted to deal with Morgan Grenfell. Given that they hadn't liked the deal in the first place, Grieveson Grant were very downbeat about our chances of raising £2 million from the market. We would have to do something called a 'vendor placing', which offered shares to an institution at a discounted rate. At the time Ratners' shares were worth around 37p, and they told me they had a client who would buy them at 22p. It seemed we didn't have much choice, but then their client pulled out and they informed us they wouldn't be able to raise the money. The deal was off.

I was desperate to secure Terry's, not just because buying a profitable chain made sound financial sense, but because I knew that we needed Terry back as our buyer. If I let this deal slip away, I felt I would be letting the whole company slip away with it. I took Terry to a meeting at Morgan Grenfell in the hope of finding a solution. I was helped by the fact that Terry was going through a difficult divorce, and he was almost as keen as I was to find a way forward so that he could reach a settlement with his wife. Roger Selig, joined us for the meeting and he kept referring to Terry as Mr Tom. Terry, understandably, was very confused.

'He does know my name, doesn't he?' he whispered to me.

I explained to him that the City always give companies code names so that if their conversations are overheard, no one knows what they're planning. Terry's code name had been Tom. It was a light-hearted moment in a very serious meeting, but whichever way we thrashed out a deal, it still involved issuing shares below their value through a vendor placing. And as Grieveson Grant couldn't find us a buyer, I really feared the deal was going to fall through.

'Why don't you just issue the shares straight to Terry?' Roger asked.

It was a perfectly reasonable question, and the answer was that it would make Terry by far the largest shareholder. I wasn't comfortable with the family losing control of the family business. Nevertheless, it was increasingly looking like my only option.

Terry and I discussed in private a deal that would work for both of us. We settled on £2.5 million in shares and a loan note for the rest. If I did this, it would dilute the holding of the other shareholders, but as the company would be worth more after the acquisition, everyone would benefit in the long term. If I wanted Terry's, then the price I would have to pay would be giving him the largest shareholding. It wasn't the deal I wanted, but we shook on it anyway.

However, it turned out that we still had one last hurdle to overcome. Terry's wife owned 27% of his company and had the right to veto any deal. I don't know the ins and outs of their divorce negotiations, but they were clearly going through a period when they couldn't agree on anything. She refused, and when Terry phoned to tell me the deal was off, I was shattered. I had put so much into reaching an agreement, and seeing it slip away was very hard to take.

'Can't we do it without her consent?' I asked Theodore Goddard, the solicitor Ratners had used for a number of years. He assured me that any deal Terry and Ratners signed wouldn't be binding without her consent.

'Is there really nothing you can say to her to make her change her mind?' I asked Terry one last time.

'I'll try again, but I don't hold out much hope.'

I don't know what he said to her, but somehow he got her to change her mind and Terry was duly issued with £2.5 million worth of shares at 30p each. A few years later, he would sell them at £4.20. It was by far the hardest deal I ever did in my career, even though it was the smallest.

Whether it was because my father really didn't want to work with Terry, or whether it was because he really was ready for retirement and wanted to spend more time with my mother, I don't know. But whatever my father's reasons were for agreeing to stand aside, it was good to know that he would be able to help my mother get treatment for her latest battle with cancer. She had been fighting the disease for over 10 years at this point, and the effort was starting to take its toll on both of them. However, my father knew too much about the business to lose him from the company completely, and so I asked him to become the non-executive chairman of the board. Having him on hand for advice and guidance was a sensible move, and despite the ructions over Terry's, my father still loved the company.

CHAPTER 10

Turnaround

When the deal had been signed, Terry Jordan walked back into Ratners' head office for a meeting with Victor and me. The meeting lasted about an hour, and in that hour, Terry earned every one of the £4 million pounds we had paid him. He talked about how to buy the best merchandise and how to get customers walking back through the door, and as he talked, Victor and I made notes. That one-hour meeting transformed our business, almost overnight.

Victor started making changes to the merchandise based on Terry's advice, and the sales figures turned around within weeks. The thing Terry made us realise was that the primary consideration when people bought jewellery was price. This was something that had really changed in the jewellery market – customers weren't looking at heirlooms, they were thinking about what they would wear that night. What Terry told us made sense: our market was primarily younger women who would make an impulse purchase and buy gold in the same way they might previously have bought plastic and costume jewellery.

We changed all our engagement rings from 18ct gold to 9ct, which nobody even noticed. Manufacturing methods were changing too, so it was possible to stamp out earrings and pendants using far less gold. Victor was now on the lookout for products that were made of lighter gold, and with real gems, but that used as little of the key ingredients as possible. Surprisingly, I don't think he ever spoke to Terry about merchandise again, but I am convinced he couldn't have made the changes without that crucial hour with Terry.

As the new production methods made earrings and chains cheaper, we moved them to the front of the window and moved our diamond rings into the arcade windows. This might sound insignificant, but it was really quite revolutionary in the jewellery business: we were hiding our prestige items and flaunting our cheaper products. What this meant was that customers walking down the high street saw a £10 pair of earrings rather than a £300 ring. Our key shopping hours became Saturday afternoons, when women would make impulse purchases they would wear that night. Saturdays became so busy that the staff often wouldn't get a moment to sit down.

With Victor and me ringing the changes, Ratners stopped being a stuffy old jewellers and turned into a trendy fashion store that had more in common with Topshop and Dorothy Perkins than a once-in-a-lifetime shop like Ernest Jones. We realised that what we were doing was turning the clock back. Our attempt to move upmarket – as every other jeweller had tried in the early Eighties – had been our undoing. Terry's had really been the old Ratners (people used to say he was wearing our old clothes), and it was clear our path now was making Ratners the new Terry's, even though we would continue to run his stores side by side with our own.

In the early Eighties, young professionals had spending power like never before, and our customers were getting younger and younger. Our posters screamed discounts and '3 for 2' offers just like the fashion shops, and we started playing music and replaced the chandeliers with modern light fittings. We were taking all the mystique out of buying jewellery and making our shops as welcoming as Marks & Spencer. Other jewellers were still looking staid and serious, and our customers were too intimidated to cross their thresholds.

It's amazing in retail how quickly you can get results: you can make a decision on a Thursday, implement the changes by Saturday, and on Monday you can check the sales figures to see the results. It is unbelievably exciting to get such instant feedback from customers, and it seemed every week we were making progress. I suppose the analogy would be a new manager taking over a failing football team: with a few changes in strategy, the same players can achieve vastly improved results.

As we were a publicly owned company, we had to publish our accounts, and when the City started to notice our sharp increase in sales and profits, Ratners came in for a fair bit of press attention. Journalists started to call me up looking for quotes about retail trends and the booming economy. I had heard cautionary tales about the British press building people up just to knock them down, but at the time I never thought there would be a downside to my relationship with the media.

Now that I was sole chief executive, I had the authority to make changes on the hoof, and I felt no need to consult with the other directors. Jack was busy with the property side of the business, and Mr Hussein could see the changes I was making were benefiting the balance sheets, so he left me alone too.

I had promoted one of our best workers, a guy called John Hughes, to be our general manager, and along with Victor, we drove through changes with astonishing speed. There was no email in those days of course, so everything was done by memo. On Monday morning we'd post out memos saying 'play music' or 'put a sandwich board on the pavement' to each of our shop managers, and by the weekend, the entire Ratners chain had made the changes. It was incredibly exciting to see ideas and plans put into action so quickly and effectively. Seeing the changes – my changes – was very satisfying. In fact it was almost addictive, and nothing in my personal life could match the thrill of turning around the business. I became incredibly single-minded, and looking back I find it hard to remember much of family life in those years. If I had paid more attention, I might have noticed that my marriage was in trouble.

John Hughes was a great facilitator, and if I asked him to do something it would be done almost immediately. I could delegate a large part of the day-to-day running of the company to him. For years, managers hadn't had someone they could call when carpet got worn out or the windows got broken. John was my Mr Fix It, and if the R in Ratners fell off in Dunfermline, he would make sure it was swiftly replaced. The managers responded well to John's efforts, and they felt their concerns were being treated seriously by head office – it was a big change from the days when everybody was scared to mention anything to my father.

When John first started, we had a series of meetings with all the managers and we told them they could say anything they liked to us. At the end of the process we had a list of about 80 complaints, ranging from the fact that the staff weren't paid enough to it taking too long for orders to be delivered. Some of them were very minor, but they added up to unnecessary inefficiencies and 700 slightly disgruntled staff. For the most part it was easy to incorporate their suggestions, and implementing their changes made them feel valued and listened to. This, combined with the upturn in sales, meant there was a good feeling in our shops: they had become fun places to work and my memories of turning up unannounced at our shops in those days are of being treated a bit like visiting royalty. The staff were pleased to see me, and I was thrilled to learn how much morale had improved, and this cycle of self-belief and positivity seemed to bring even better results.

The turnaround meant we were able to pay people a little bit more and start to expand again. We opened 30 stores in 1984 and 1985, creating hundreds of opportunities for promotions and pay rises. Everyone in the organisation felt like they were working for a company that was going places, and their levels of enthusiasm and commitment soared.

Uncle Jack was still the head of our property department, although by this stage he had a very able assistant called Simon Taylor. Simon was more my age, and he knew that part of the reason behind Ratners' struggles had been the fact that we had been absent from shopping malls. For two decades since our flop in Birmingham's Bullring, we had missed out on the biggest change in retailing in a century. With my father now out of the office, we started trying to make up for lost time and get into as many shopping centres as possible. My father had never changed his mind about them, despite the fact that other jewellers had some of their most successful stores in shopping malls.

I was so desperate to get us into shopping centres that I told Simon I was happy to pay full price for the right units. Sometimes I would go and look at the unit before we agreed to take it, usually on a Saturday afternoon, but I was so busy in the mid-Eighties that I couldn't always spare the time. Once we had secured the shop, a very well-oiled machine went into action. Alan Godden, our shop fitter, would come to my office and I would sketch out the shop layout with him. I would get out my ruler and start drawing it to scale – I knew exactly where I wanted the gold window, or how long the arcade should be. Occasionally there'd be a column or a girder that would have to be worked round, but 95% of what I drew at those meetings ended up in the shops. It was something my father had done before me, and it felt good to be taking on this particular role from him.

The shops were rolled out with a McDonalds approach – every shop had the same stock, the same lettering on the facia, the same tills. In a sense, everything was just off-the-shelf, so we could actually open a shop without having to design anything bespoke. If we were opening in Cardiff or Swansea or Luton, it was essentially the same shop.

Alan would deal with the planning departments of local councils for us, but we became so adept at knowing what would and would not get planning that we started to fit out shops without the relevant paperwork. It was a foolish thing to do, but I was impatient to make Ratners the biggest jeweller in the world. We were still using my father's photo system for the window displays, so it was a bit like painting by numbers for the new managers – they received their display pads and their merchandise and just had to follow the photos. It was incredibly simple, and therefore incredibly effective.

The new managers – usually newly promoted from another store – were empowered to hire their own staff, and as long as they were neatly presented, they worked hard, and the stock was always polished and gleaming, head office rarely interfered with their choices. This meant we had a very young, very vibrant workforce and you could sense the moment you walked into a Ratners shop that you weren't in a stuffy jewellers. I had people in the industry come up to me at that point and tell me, 'you have completely ruined your father's business'. I just smiled at them and said, 'that must be why sales are up 50 per cent'.

It was clear the changes I had implemented had made a huge difference, and I didn't see the point of bringing in consultants and agents to oversee the transition. I was actually very anti using outside agencies because I felt we were more qualified to run our business than an outsider. I knew that H. Samuel had spent a fortune bringing in all kinds of 'experts', and not only had they not made any changes that had increased their profits, they had diverted the executives away from running the business and had wasted their time.

H. Samuel was actually making quite a few mistakes at this point, and I can't deny it gave me pleasure to see our sales soar as theirs declined. They had recently hired a new chief executive – in the Eighties the title of Managing Director was no longer flash enough – from Dixons. He'd been brilliant in electronics, but he knew nothing about the jewellery business and they really lost their way.

I first realised just how much trouble they were in when I visited our shop in Ballymena in Northern Ireland in the run-up to Christmas. The H. Samuel shop was round the corner from ours and I was curious to see it because I knew they'd hired a big design consultancy to do their Christmas displays. As soon as I saw their window, I knew they were going to have a bad Christmas. They had stuck plastic icicles over the windows so that you couldn't see the jewellery! When I was a lot younger, I'd learnt a valuable lesson in sales when I'd gone to Petticoat Lane market. I'd noticed that it didn't really matter who had the best gear, it was the stallholders who shouted the loudest that got the most sales. If you compared Ratners' windows that Christmas – which were full of posters for and cheap merchandise – with H. Samuel's windows, it was as if they were just whispering to their customers to come in while we were screaming from the top of our lungs.

Samuel's had let the designers have full rein, and they had forgotten some of the basic rules of selling jewellery window layouts. For instance, if you look at most successful jewellers, you'll notice how the diamond rings are – almost always – precisely 42″ from the ground. Bizarre as this may sound, there's a very good reason for it: the average woman is 5′4″, and if a ring is 42″ from the ground, it will be in her eye line. H. Samuel's designers had put the diamond rings above head height. It was clear their fortunes were not about to change and their share price would continue to drop. I'm not quite sure when I first had the thought that I might try and buy H. Samuel, but it might well have been that day in Ballymena.

CHAPTER 11

The Big Time

Ratners had come a long way in a very short space of time, but our success wasn't unusual. This was the Eighties, and the papers were full of junk bond traders making millions overnight and entrepreneurs like Alan Sugar and Richard Branson living extravagant lifestyles. Just as the shoulder pads got bigger in our suits, so did our deals. It was the era of smaller companies doing audacious takeovers. There was WPP, a small award-winning advertising company who bid for J. Walter Thompson, who were much bigger than them, Saatchi's bid for an American company called Ted Bates, and Iceland took over Beejam. The City was in deal mode, and there was money to be made.

In the Seventies, stockbrokers had been looking for 10% growth from the big, dependable businesses like GUS and ICI, but those corporate giants had gone out of fashion and the Saatchi's, the Ratners, and the Carltons became hot property, in part because they were headed by young men. There were lots of articles in the papers about 'Forty to watch under 40', and the City was seeking out young, aggressive entrepreneurs who were not afraid to buy huge businesses. They were able to do this because their shares were doubling inside 12 months. This came on the back of hype created by young analysts – the typical red braces-wearing young hustler from movies like *Wall Street* – who were talking up the companies, and increasing their forecasts to ridiculous levels. Looking back, it should have been easy to predict that a recession wouldn't be too many years behind, because you shouldn't run a business chasing brokers' forecasts, you should take a long-term view. But this was the Eighties, and people were only interested in the here and now. This was an era when flamboyant and exciting operators were seizing their moment, and as the decade went on, perhaps the most audacious takeover was Charles Saatchi's announcement that he intended to buy the Midland Bank! He was an advertising expert, not a banker, so perhaps it was not surprising that his bid ultimately failed.

Ratners' rapid turnaround had created a lot of interest in the media, and I had been forced to hire an outside PR agency to handle all the interview requests. I was learning that the press could be very useful, and I discussed how I might let it be known that I wanted to buy H. Samuel without seeming arrogant or ridiculous. My PR agent arranged an interview with one of the *Daily Telegraph*'s business correspondents, David Brewerton, and as working in a broom cupboard above the shop no longer created the right impression, I took him to Mark's – a private club in Charles Street – for lunch. Journalists are always looking for stories that are bigger than a deal their rivals have written about, and so I let David know just how well we were doing – our shares were worth three times what they'd been at the beginning of 1984 and we'd just announced annual profits of £2.2 million, which was a doubling of the previous figure – and talked about how much H. Samuel was underperforming. He then followed the logic and wrote in the following day's paper that Ratners should buy Samuel's. And as it looked like his suggestion, it gave my plans even more credence.

He knew, as did I, that the City had wanted changes at Samuel's for some time. It had an archaic share structure that was seen as a barrier to investors turning a decent profit. Samuel's shareholding was made up of A and B shares. The A shares represented about £13 million and were owned by the Edgar family, the relatives of the original founders. The B shares – which represented about £125 million and around 73% of the stock – were publicly owned but didn't have the same voting rights as the A shares. So although the Edgars only owned 37% of the value of H. Samuel, the voting structure meant they had over 50% of the votes at board meetings.

I had no doubt that the City would be behind my bid, but was pleasantly surprised to learn that many of the Edgar family felt that way too. A large proportion of the A shares were still owned by aunts, uncles, and cousins of the man in charge, Anthony Edgar, who was the son of the founder. Being the sort of family they were, they read the *Telegraph* and David Brewerton's suggestion had hit the right note. For the past couple of years they had seen Tony Dignum, the chief executive who had been such a success at Dixons, oversee a period of relative decline at H. Samuel. Many family members could see that under the current management, it was entirely possible that the value of their shares could fall even further. Several of these relatives had also fallen out with Anthony Edgar over the appointment of Tony Dignum and they just wanted out.

I received a phone call from Morgan Grenfell, the merchant bank I'd used on the Terry's deal, saying they had been approached by family members who had read the article in the *Telegraph* and wanted to sell their shares. Their holding represented 27% of the A shares, and Morgan Grenfell negotiated to buy them for £7 million cash. It was a relatively small amount of money to effectively buy a quarter of the voting rights of a £150 million company. I'm not sure if the Edgars realised it at the time, but their share structure really backfired on them. As one commentator said at the time, I had bought my stake for 'a mere bagatelle'. And as Ratners was now so profitable, I actually had £7 million in the bank. While the deal made some members of the Edgar family very happy, I knew there would be one Edgar who would resist my advances.

I had known Anthony Edgar for many years – we'd often run into each other – and I knew that although we had a lot in common (namely that we both ran our father's jewellery businesses), we weren't very alike. Ratners was down-to-earth and Samuel's had pretensions to be something better, and I think that probably went for our personalities too. At 45, he was only 10 years older than me, but he behaved like he was from another generation. He was the kind of guy who wore plus fours to play golf and went shooting at the weekend. I knew that telling him an upstart like me wanted to take over his business wouldn't go down well, so when I walked into his office for a meeting, I took a different tack.

'I think we should merge.'

I talked about all the market advantages we would have, the economies of scale, and the reductions in overheads, but he didn't want to hear any of it.

'I don't want to merge with you.' He said this in a way that made Ratners sound like it was the shit on Samuel's shoe. The Edgars also owned the prestigious Watches of Switzerland chain that sold £500,000 Patek Philippe pocket watches: he really didn't think I was fit to own any of his company. 'You may have 27 per cent of the shares now, but all that lets you do is attend the AGM and put your hand up and vote. It doesn't give you any power because I still own 30 per cent and my mother owns 11 per cent.'

So of course one of the first phone calls I made after that meeting was to Morgan Grenfell.

'His mother owns 11 per cent. Do you think she'd sell?' I asked.

The brokers set up a meeting with her, and when I met her a few weeks later I thought she was like some dowager duchess out of Jeeves and Wooster – not the kind of person I was used to dealing with at all. After a suitable amount of small talk, I brought up the idea of a merger.

'Oh yes, I've been reading a bit about that. I think that's a marvellous idea. There's just one thing...'

'Yes?'

'Well, I'm not really all that sure that Anthony should run the merged company. He's totally unsuitable really. Don't you think?'

I was stunned but tried very hard to keep a straight face. After that, negotiating to buy her shares was pretty straightforward – I knew our profits meant that borrowing the money would be easy – and of course that would mean I had more shares than Anthony. Naturally

I leaked this little matter to the press, and slowly the pressure on him started to build. It became clear that the City had lost faith in him and Tony Dignum, and their share price began to tumble, which made them very vulnerable to a takeover. Tony had also become a bit of a laughing stock when his affair with their marketing manager, (the person who had been responsible for their awful icicle window displays), became public, making him even more unpopular with the upper-crust Edgars. H. Samuel desperately needed some credibility, and suddenly a merger sounded like a good option. It was a week before Samuel's was due to announce its annual profits when my phone finally rang: it was Anthony Edgar wanting to negotiate the terms of a merger. We made an appointment for the following week to talk over the details.

Had I been playing snooker with Charles and Michael that afternoon, it would have been a good time to brag a bit and make jokes at the others' expense. In less than two years as chief executive, I had transformed Ratners: we had a market capitalisation – i.e. the value of all our shares – of £40 million, we had 180 shops and our share price was now nudging the £2 mark. Despite all this, I had only been paying myself a salary of £35,000, and I knew that when the ink was dry on the Samuel's deal, I could put a zero on the end of that figure. I had every reason to feel ecstatic.

I went home that night on a high. We had not long moved to a fantastic house in Highgate overlooking Kenwood on Hampstead Heath, and as I parked in the driveway and locked my Porsche, I think I probably thought I had it made. However that night, when the kids had gone to bed, Angela told me she wanted a divorce.

CHAPTER 12

Trauma

Over the next few days, we talked about why she had made such a decision, and if I'm honest it was the first time we had spoken properly in years. She was fed up with me coming home late, of not being able to talk to me because I was too tired, or of me reading the paper when I could have been helping out with domestic matters, and of being short-tempered when she asked for help.

'You're always in your own world', she said, 'so we might as well be apart'.

There was another thing that neither of us could bring ourselves to say: we had fallen out of love.

In those few days after her announcement I was almost dizzy, practically sick, with conflicting emotions: I was euphoric about the Samuel's deal, but so shell-shocked by Angela's announcement, guilty about my negligence, and worried about the impact it would have on my children, who were only 12 and 10 years old at the time. I didn't know what I would do or how I would feel from one moment to the next. On top of this, Angela made it clear she wanted me to move out, which meant I would be homeless. I agreed to check into a hotel, but was adamant that we weren't going to tell the children: Angela had threatened divorce a few times in the past and I was hopeful I would be able to persuade her I could be a better husband. It didn't help my mood to know my daughters were unlikely to ask the 'where's daddy' question because they would barely notice my absence.

When I checked into the hotel, I felt drained. I had barely eaten for three or four days and I felt incredibly weak. I sat alone in that room and thought about everything I had just walked away from and got this overwhelming sense that my life was over. It may never have been the greatest marriage, but it was *my* marriage, and for the past 14 years I had loved the stability and order it had given my life. I had loved having the kids and their friends running around the house, I had loved my Saturdays out with the girls, and I had loved our new home. In my way, I had also loved Angela too.

A couple of days later, I turned up for my meeting with Anthony Edgar at what was called H. Samuel's 'head office'. In effect it was Anthony's home – a fabulous town house in Arlington Street – but as it was company property it had to be used for business occasionally to keep the taxman happy. I had been told by his assistant to arrive at 7 o'clock, so that's when I rang the bell. His wife Sarah answered the door, and she was very good at the small talk and pleasantries.

'You're looking well Gerald. Lost a bit of weight?'

'I'm on a diet', I lied, as I refused another tray of canapés. I still couldn't bring myself to eat.

'Anthony won't be long. Make yourself at home.'

He turned up half an hour later as he'd gone for a drink in the Blue Lamp pub opposite the house. I realise now that I rarely saw him sober. He was accompanied by his personal accountant, and they quickly told me that they would agree to a merger – subject to a few loose ends being tidied up, of course.

'What do you think we should call the new company?' he asked.

'I don't know.'

'Well we think we should call it H. Samuel Ratners.'

'OK.'

Some people are surprised I didn't put up a fight about the name, but the truth is I really didn't care. It had been my ambition to make Ratners the biggest jeweller in the country, and with this merger I would have achieved that. The merger sent us into the big league: we would have a combined market capitalisation of £190 million, we would be leaping from 180 shops to over 600, and we would own some of the most valuable retail real estate in the country because Samuel's owned the freeholds of 50 per cent of their shops.

I also had a plan that meant I would be in control. So when Anthony insisted on being chairman, I said that was fine, as long as I was chief executive. I had a hunch that the City wouldn't stand for such an incompetent chairman for long, and felt sure that I wouldn't be working with him for ever. His next condition was that he should be allowed to bring his board members with him. Samuel's board only had three members, so I agreed to that, just so long as I could bring four of my own board members. He smarted a little at this, but Ratners had six people on its board and asking two of them to step aside would be difficult enough. So long as I had more people on the board than he did, then I didn't care about anything else: I would have control over the merged company, and that's all I wanted.

I should have been delighted, but returning to the hotel that night was terrible: I should have been celebrating, but instead I was on my own and beginning to feel increasingly isolated. I knew I had to eat something, but I just didn't have an appetite.

The three Ratners board members I wanted, in addition to myself, were Victor, Mr Hussein, and a new finance director I had hired from Morgan Grenfell called Andrew Coppell. That meant I would have to ask my father and my uncle to step down from the board. They were both difficult conversations.

I went to see my father at his house. Of course, my mother was there too – they were still inseparable – so I said to him 'I would like to talk to you without my mother', because I knew my mother would tell everybody and it was still top secret at that stage. (Of course my father went and told my mother straight away anyway, so the secrecy didn't count for anything.) We went upstairs to one of the bedrooms. His whole house was an oddity of antiques and this room didn't have furniture you could actually call a chair, so he perched on an old

Chinese porcelain drum while I spoke. The whole place was stuffed with pieces he'd bought at Portobello Road. Anyway, I told him about the deal.

'Are you sure Anthony Edgar wants to do the deal?'

'Of course.'

'It's just that I was at Brent Cross the other day, and I was looking in our window. It looked like a market stall with all those posters and watches hanging down from the ceiling. Are you sure he wants to be associated with a business like that?'

'Yes, Dad. I'm absolutely sure. But the reason I'm here is… Well, it's about the board…'

He understood my reasons for wanting him to stand aside, and when my brother-in-law, Denise's husband, who was a stockbroker, predicted the merger could see our share price hit £10, my father became far more enthusiastic about the deal.

He quickly realised the merger was good for Ratners and I think he was proud of my achievements. He recognised that he hadn't played a role in our recent success, and to his credit he agreed that it was the right time to step aside. He'd also read the papers and knew what the press were saying about me, about how I'd led the company out of the wilderness, and I think he realised he didn't have much left to offer the company. His shares were now worth millions more than they had been when he'd stepped down as joint MD two years ago, and so he knew his retirement would be well funded. Jack's shares also meant he could live in luxury for the rest of his life, but he said he wasn't quite ready to retire. He graciously stepped down from the board, but continued to work on the property side of things. They both wished me luck, and it was wonderful to know that they would still be on the other end of a phone if I ever needed some advice. In some ways, this had been a real rite of passage: the baton had been handed from one generation to the next and it felt great to know I was carrying on the family business and making Ratners a household name.

My home life was still a mess, however. Although I hadn't given up hope of a reconciliation with Angela, she had and wanted to tell the children. We were both petrified of how they would react and so Angela consulted a psychologist who gave her advice about the best way to break such news to a child. We were told that we should both be there when they heard our announcement and that it was advisable that they were told on neutral ground: if they learnt such devastating news in their bedroom they might not settle in that room again.

So Angela and I went through the farce of telling Suzy that it was a nice day and that we should all go for a walk. I can't remember where Lisa was – she might have been staying with a friend – so the three of us went for a walk on Hampstead Heath. Telling her we were divorcing was the single worst moment of my life up until that point: I felt like a failure, and I was filled with this dreadful sense that I had let her down. Thankfully she had some friends whose parents were divorced, and this helped her accept what we were telling her. I still feel awful about it to this day.

As long as I was living in a hotel, I couldn't have my daughters to visit me. Not seeing them was having a devastating effect on me, so much so that friends and colleagues started to comment on my deterioration. At work, Victor and the other directors insisted that I went and got help: I got to the stage where I was so upset I couldn't concentrate on anything other than my divorce. I was incapable of work and so Victor suggested I take some leave – something pretty unheard of. I checked myself into a health farm for a couple of weeks where my diet would be monitored, and I would be forced to rest.

It was odd to be away from both family and business: it had never happened before, and I realised how lost I was without them. Gradually I began to feel my strength come back and came to a level of acceptance about my marriage ending that allowed me to function again. When I returned to London, my priority was finding somewhere to live, but as I secretly had hopes of rebuilding my marriage, I didn't want to take on a tenancy anywhere as I felt that would send out the wrong signals to Angela and the kids.

The Loftus family, who owned Accurist watches, heard about my situation and offered to let me use a flat of theirs off Baker Street. I accepted like a shot and only later found out what a depressing place it was. I was kept awake most nights as it was right next to the fire station and there were sirens going off throughout the night. It was also decorated in a very Eighties fashion – everything was black and white and all the seats were leather – there wasn't a warm surface in the flat. It was a typical bachelor pad and there were no homely touches, not even any pictures on the wall. I was so miserable there that I longed for my beautiful home in Highgate. I felt so alone that I would happily have given up the H. Samuel deal if it had somehow meant I could have gone home: in my mind, the day I had gained one I had lost the other and it seemed pretty obvious to me that the two events were linked. My only comfort was that now that I had my own place, Suzy and Lisa could come and stay. Of course, I was so guilt-ridden, that I had to make every day I spent with them as special as possible and our days out got grander and grander.

Dealing with the merger consumed much of my time in the following months. Suddenly there were hundreds of new stores to visit and thousands of employees to meet. We had a series of meetings with all the shop managers and told them that we were going to make big investments in their shop fronts – which had been neglected for years – and were going to give them merchandise that they could actually sell. We also said that we were going to pay them a little bit more and bring in some extra staff. Naturally, this went down incredibly well, and when I finished my little speech I said, 'Now I want you to tell me what you'd like to see changed.' I made a note of 93 suggestions, and at the end of the meeting I told them that I was going to go away and deal with every single one of them. When Victor and I got up to leave, the managers actually applauded: it seemed they'd never had senior management take such an interest in what they did before.

I got a real kick out of visiting Samuel's stores because they were so glamorous. We were still running the Terry's stores, and because they'd been opened very cheaply they didn't have any facilities. If you asked to use the loo in one of them, the staff would give you directions to public toilets at the other end of the high street: in Samuel's stores they asked if you wanted Ladies or Gents. I couldn't quite believe that I owned them. This was the company my parents had held up as the benchmark when we'd talked about the business over dinner. Now they were part of Ratners.

Of course, merging two companies, with two cultures and two staffs, wasn't without its problems, but by far the biggest battles were at board level. I remember going to visit Samuel's factory in Birmingham. Anthony Edgar had offered to show us around our new asset, and as he was giving us the tour he looked at Victor and said:

'Take your hands out of your pockets.'

He was even ruder than my father but he didn't have the excuse of having had brain surgery. I had a series of meetings with City investors in those first few months to reassure them about the debt we had taken on to secure the merger, and somehow Anthony knew whenever I was with them. A secretary would always knock at the door and say, 'There's a call for you Mr Ratner.' Often Anthony was incoherent and just wanted to tell me he was at the Henley Regatta or Ascot, or some other function. Even when I was visiting the shops, a man would come up to me with a note to say there was an urgent phone call. He clearly couldn't stand me running the company and wanted to find ways of letting me know he was still around.

I found his behaviour intolerable and completely unacceptable as the chairman of a publicly owned company. I felt I had no choice but to take legal advice about removing him. Lawyers are paid to be cautious, which meant I wasn't told what I wanted to hear.

'You'll have to be careful. If it looks like you entered into the merger under false pretences, he could sue you. He could reasonably say your intentions were a takeover and that's not what he agreed to.'

'But I cannot work with this man. Isn't there anything I can do?'

My lawyer thought about this for a while. 'Well, if you can prove that you've worked with him for three months and have found the situation untenable, then you might just get away with removing him.'

My definition of untenable and the law's definition of untenable were slightly different, so I had no choice but to suffer his interference for a couple more months. When the time limit was up, I went to see Anthony and told him that it wasn't working. 'You'll have to go', I said, knowing full well he wouldn't go quietly. A substantial payoff helped though.

Once Anthony had left, it seemed daft to have his board members on our payroll so I approached them both – one was his personal solicitor, the other his private accountant – and told them that I saw no point in them continuing. I was worried that the lawyer might find a loophole, but he didn't want to stay without Anthony anyway. The accountant suggested that he could become the finance director, but I told him that I already had one of those.

The news of Anthony's departure was greeted enthusiastically by the City, as was the announcement that I would become chairman *and* chief executive. My dual role allowed me to increase our rate of expansion and implement changes at remarkable speed. One of the first things we did was change the merchandise in H. Samuel stores. Many years previously, I had said that I thought Samuel's shops were too big and that they had to fill their shelves with gifts. I still hated the gift side of their business, so I took the opportunity to get rid of the stock. We announced a 'takeover sale' and put posters with impressive flags in the windows (Samuel's was far too classy for a downmarket poster). Everything was reduced by 50%, and with that kind of discount we sold stock that had been sitting on the shelves for years.

Victor did exactly what he'd done in the Ratners stores – he brought in stock that was made more cheaply, but looked just as good, that we could sell for less. In many cases the stock was identical to jewellery sold in Ratners shops, and because H. Samuel had bigger shops in better positions, the volume of trade was phenomenal. If you took the Ratners shop in Croydon, it might sell 20 pairs of a particular earring on a Saturday afternoon, but the Samuel's store in the same town might sell 100 of them. It was only really then that I understood just what a good and respected brand H. Samuel had been. In the public's mind, it was up there with Boots and Marks & Spencer.

The combination of Ratners' marketing expertise, the right products, and H. Samuel's reputation was a winning combination. The mid-Eighties were a boom time for most retailers, but we were starting to report fabulous 50% and 60% increases in profits, and as a consequence our shares rocketed – in 1986, Ratners stock went up more than any other share – eventually hitting £4 a share in April 1987. We became such a slick operation that it seemed ridiculous we were still running our factory in Camden, as well as the Samuel's factory in Birmingham. I had wanted to shut the factory down for over a decade, and now I finally sold it off.

The turnaround in Ratners' fortunes was so dramatic that I started to come in for a lot of attention personally, and in 1986 I was made Retailer of the Year. I know it's a bit of a cliché, but it really is terrific when you've been chosen by your peers for this kind of honour, especially when the other nominees had included Terence Conran, Ralph Halpern, and George Davies from the Next group. Accepting the award was one of the highlights of my career, and it added to the sensation that I could walk on water. It felt like everything was going my way and when someone at the awards ceremony told me to be careful – like some prophecy in a Greek tragedy, they told me that those who are fêted are eventually brought down – I thought they were talking absolute nonsense.

I got plenty of invites in those days to some of the most exclusive events, and I met some of the most famous people in the world at parties and premières. As I was well known for being wealthy, many of those invites were to charity balls and auctions. At one of them I found myself seated next to Prince Charles, which was obviously very prestigious and I have to confess to being pathetically impressed by this. However, at the end of the evening, my mood had cooled slightly: he'd requested a vegetable meal, and of course, being the Prince of Wales, the chef had gone to town preparing a sumptuous *vegetarian* meal.

'But I said I wanted vegetables, not all this nonsense.'

It reminded me of being with my father! Thankfully I didn't have to go to these events on my own, as I had unexpectedly found myself in a new relationship. I had first met Moira Day when she came in for an interview to be my secretary. She was much younger than me and, of course, I had no romantic thoughts about her at first, I had simply been impressed by her CV and she had interviewed well. But when I offered her the job, she turned me down: she'd been offered a promotion by her employer, a perfume business in Curzon Street. I wasn't going to take 'no' for an answer, so I went to see her and offered her a pay increase and a company car, and this persuaded her to come and work with me.

When she first started at Ratners, I was in a terrible state. I was living in the Loftus' flat off Baker Street and tentatively negotiating my divorce. I was probably working 18-hour days at the time, which didn't leave a lot of time for eating or sleeping. I'd thrown myself into work because I was completely unable to organise my personal life: for 15 years Angela had done everything and I didn't have a clue about getting laundry done or supermarket shopping or even who I needed to call to sort out paying the electricity bill. I was really quite terrified: I ran a huge business but I couldn't handle my personal life. When I was at home, I was too scared to go out, and yet if I had to sit in on my own in that dark flat on a Sunday afternoon, I felt I would die. Moira recognised I was in a mess and took charge of my home life as well as my office. She arranged for a daily woman to come and clean and bought things I needed – like teabags and a pint of milk.

She was a rock for me in those days, and even though I was 35 and she was 24, she didn't mind hanging out with me. We started running together on Sunday mornings in the park, and then we started going to galleries together in the afternoons. It took a while for me to realise that I was falling in love, and after the galleries, we would go for dinner. Of course, like most couples, there would be spats, but unlike most couples we worked together, so things would occasionally get tense in the office. We broke things off once or twice in the early days as we negotiated our working relationship, but 21 years and two kids later, we're still together.

CHAPTER 13

Thatcher's Decade

Of all the invites I received in the late Eighties, the one that excited me the most was a request to join Margaret Thatcher for a private lunch at Number 10. I had been there several times for receptions and 'fact-finding' lunches, but a private lunch was something only very influential people were invited to. Or so I thought at the time: in reality it was probably a 'thank you' for a donation I had made to the Conservative party. It wasn't a big one – £25,000 – but no doubt they hoped a bit of flattery might get me to open my cheque book again.

My family had always voted Conservative. There was no such thing as New Labour when I was a child and politics was simple: Labour was for the unions, the Tories were for business. As the owners of a growing business, my parents' politics was never in doubt, and neither was that of any of our friends. In the Sixties, they watched in horror as the economy was mismanaged, and cursed as Wilson lied that the 'pound in our pockets' wouldn't be affected by devaluation. Denis Healey had told Parliament that inflation was only 8%, when in real terms it had been something like 38%. With figures – both political and numeric – like those, politics had been a major part of the Ratner family's conversations over the dinner table.

I always paid attention to the budget, as I knew how it affected our family. In the Sixties, purchase tax on jewellery was at 55% because the unions saw it as a luxury for the rich. It had nearly crippled

Ratners, and in our household Labour were always spoken of as the enemy. Under the Heath government in the early Seventies, we had a ludicrous situation with the unions where they were demanding 38% salary rises and the Labour party were backing their claim. No one in my family could see how anyone could justify such a demand, and of course when these pay claims were awarded it brought the government to its knees, and by the middle of the decade we ended up with the three-day week.

When Margaret Thatcher promised to be tough with the unions, I wasn't the only one rooting for her to win the election in 1979. When she came to power, she lowered income tax – which, let's not forget, had been at 83% and an eye-watering 98% on income from investments – and this rocket-powered the economy. With Nigel Lawson as Chancellor, the growth was phenomenal and shares started to boom. It made such a difference from the days of Healey promising to 'squeeze the rich till their pips squeak'. Under Thatcher's leadership, Britain leapt up all sorts of league tables, from productivity to investment to education – we even started getting good at football again – so it was fair to say I was a big fan of the Iron Lady.

I was asked to make a donation by the then Treasurer of the Conservatives, Sir Hector Lang, who was also the MD of United Biscuits. We had met at a lunch organised by the *Evening Standard* at which I'd been presented with the Young Businessman of the Year award. We'd got on well and made each other laugh, and so I'd said I would write to him.

'Can you write?' he joked. He really thought I was a bit of an upstart with no education. Nevertheless, my money was as good as any Eton boy's, and a few days later he turned up at my office and told me the Conservatives were looking for donations to fight the 1987 election. I gave him a company cheque, and when Mr Hussein found the bank statements he came in to see me.

'I don't think that will look very good in the annual reports', he said. 'We'll put it down as advertising.'

And in a way, it was good for my profile, so maybe Mr Hussein was right to call it advertising. All I knew was that a few months later, an invitation arrived from Number 10. Of course, I was terribly excited but when I told Michael and Charles about it over a game of snooker, they weren't overly impressed: Michael had already been invited – whenever I have tried to boast to Michael it has been in vain – and Charles knew her very well from the days when he'd handled the Conservatives' advertising. I hadn't realised at the time that it would be such a small gathering – just me, her, Denis, and three other high-profile businessmen including David Wolfson from Great Universal Stores.

When I arrived, we stood around making small talk, although Margaret Thatcher's small talk always had an angle. I remember she asked how our shops in Northern Ireland were doing and was intrigued to hear they were among our most profitable branches. She said she was surprised because she didn't think the Irish worked very hard!

I couldn't quite tell if she was being deliberately derogatory, or if this was a joke. We were then ushered into a dining room and I was stunned to see I had been seated next to her. I went to pick up the little leather place name holder to check there wasn't a mistake when a private secretary told me discreetly that 'one isn't meant to touch the place card, only to look at it'. It was a long way from Hendon to Downing Street!

For reasons I couldn't work out, Denis was acting as some sort of chairman and all the questions had to go through him. But if he then said too much he was told, promptly, to shut up!

'Denis. Denis! I would like to ask Mr Ratner where he thinks the high street is going.'

I knew she was worried about inflation because Britain was having such a boom and the Treasury was trying to control it by putting interest rates up. Looking back, I realise I was there to tell them if the high street was cooling so she could avoid the politically difficult decision to raise interest rates again. Unfortunately for her, I could only tell her that business had never been better.

She was then called away and was gone for 20 minutes. When she returned she explained that there had been a murder in Northern Ireland and she insisted on being informed of news from the province as soon as it happened. It was fascinating to see how discreetly and efficiently Number 10 worked, and of course, as she had a packed timetable to keep to, it meant lunch was wrapped up shortly after she returned.

I found her personally very impressive. Everyone who worked with her looked up to her and she commanded respect, even from her enemies. She had replaced Ted Heath as party leader who hadn't had the personal leadership qualities she possessed, and you could tell the party was grateful to her for returning them to power so convincingly. I've since read that several of her cabinet ministers actually found her attractive: I can't say I fancied her when I met her, but when she was younger she was a good-looking woman. Michael said the same when he met her: there was something undeniably appealing about her in those days. I could certainly understand how she made many people feel tongue-tied and stupid, but the thing I liked about her the most was that she remained down-to-earth. She was still a Grantham shop keeper's daughter, although by the end of her premiership I think the power had started to corrupt, and that's when she lost her charm.

I was invited back on a number of occasions, and many of the people I met at Number 10 – like Richard Branson and Geoff Mulcahy of the Kingfisher group – ended up with knighthoods. If I was being uncharitable, I'd guess maybe they'd given party donations of a lot more than £25,000!

I had a pretty extravagant lifestyle in those days. I had moved into the house in Arlington Street that had been Anthony Edgar's before the takeover. It felt a little odd taking the guy's house as well as his company, but it was in the West End right next door to Le Caprice restaurant. As I couldn't carry on living in the basement flat without becoming morbidly depressed, it seemed crazy not to move in. Most importantly, it was somewhere lovely for my daughters to come and visit me.

I didn't care much for Anthony Edgar's taste in interiors, so I arranged for some designers to come and give me their ideas. I picked one I liked and told them to get on with it. There was no budget. I didn't even ask for a budget, and I didn't question the bill when it arrived. The more that was spent, the better as far as I was concerned. My salary was probably £500,000 a year back then, which would be more like £900,000 today, and as I had used share options to buy as much Ratners stock as I could, I also had assets of £7 or £8 million. On top of this, the company paid for most of my expenses, so I had an amazing lifestyle.

Oddly though, it didn't make me all that happy: for some reason it didn't mean much to me. I remember sitting watching the budget at the house in Arlington Street and hearing the then Chancellor, Nigel Lawson, announcing that he was reducing the top rate of tax from 60% to 40%. On my earnings I would be over £100,000 a year better off: it should have been like winning the lottery, but it didn't do anything for me. I asked myself why, and realised that I was still very traumatised by the breakdown of my marriage. Despite my new relationship with Moira, I remained in a very low place for two years after my split from Angela.

No matter how rich we became, or where our careers took us, Michael, Charles, and I rarely missed our snooker sessions. We were all at the height of our careers and could have afforded to have pool halls built in our gardens, but several times a week we would turn up at my parents' house in Regent's Park and play snooker in the basement. It was a little like being in a separate flat down there, and so that my parents weren't too disturbed, Charles arranged for his favourite deli to deliver sandwiches through the little window at pavement level.

The three of us would discuss the economy (of course Charles had no idea at this point that Nigel Lawson would one day become his father-in-law), deals we were considering, and strategies for staying on top of the competition. We took the piss out of each other as well – Charles was known as a bit of a Howard Hughes figure who hated being seen in public, and we'd tease him about never using the main entrance to his own offices or threaten to take a photograph of him and give it to the press. We were incredibly competitive and always arguing about who was the best snooker player, or the best tennis player, or who had the best clothes. One day Charles turned up with a massive silver trophy – bigger than the European Cup – that he had named the GRASA cup after the first letters of our surnames. If you won 20 games, then you won the cup. But of course as soon as one of us won it, then the other two wanted it, so I think we must have played for that cup about 50 times!

The boiler was in the snooker room, and it used to get unbearably hot in summer. The only way to keep the windows open was by jamming them with snooker cues. The boiler got in the way of our cueing action in one corner of the table, and so Charles would always try and leave the cue ball in that corner so you'd fluff your shot. We took the snooker very seriously, so whenever I took a shot, they'd say something like 'is that a bald patch?', or when Charles was lining up a pot I'd say, 'Isn't Tim Bell doing well these days.' Tim Bell, now Sir Tim, had taken over the Tories' advertising from Saatchi's. If it was a really crucial shot, then a bit of bragging would be called for. Charles once timed his announcement about buying the Midland Bank to perfectly put Michael off his stroke.

We also made ridiculous bets with each other. One night we started bragging about who knew the best routes through the backstreets of North London, and as Charles and I both lived in St John's Wood, we decided to race each other. Of course that wasn't enough of a bet for me.

'I could beat you driving backwards.'

'You're on!'

So I got in my Corniche, put it into reverse, and drove from Regent's Park to St John's Wood backwards. Charles laughed so much that I think he couldn't concentrate on driving and I did actually beat him!

It wasn't just the sandwiches that would be delivered to our snooker den. We spent so much time there – sometimes it would be five after-noons a week – that staff at Michael and Charles' offices knew where to find them, and occasionally a secretary would stand on the pavement outside my parents' house and shove some paperwork through the window for one of us to sign. It saved them having to go through all the pleasantries and explanations with my parents, so they'd just tap on the window and we'd sign whatever needed to be signed.

The mood was slightly different when Charles couldn't make it. Michael is a very good friend to talk to, and he had divorced his wife at the same time as I had split from Angela – being able to talk to someone close so openly helped us both.

The three of us listened and learned from each other, our friendship – and our rivalry – was a key factor in all our careers. On Mondays, when the *Financial Times* printed the market capitalisation figures, I would look at Ratners' market cap, but next would always be Carlton and Saatchi's before I looked at the rest of the retailers. When my market cap went above theirs, I used to underline it and send them a copy of the paper. Later, when technology moved on, I customised the computer display in my office to show real-time share information for Ratners, Carlton and Saatchi's. John Jay, the *Sunday Times* business correspondent, once came into my office and wondered why I would have two such random companies on my screen. 'You're not planning a takeover are you?' he asked, looking for a scoop. To my knowledge, although the three of us were ambitious, we never actually planned that kind of coup.

Ratners continued to perform strongly, and the City was pushing me to expand even further. Agreeing to meet brokers' growth forecasts is a bit like making a pact with the devil. The rewards are enormous in terms of bonuses and share options, but the pressure can take its toll in terms of bad decisions or growth at the expense of consolidation. But this was the Eighties, and it was all about growth, and executives like me who could deliver it were treated like royalty, and once you had a reputation like mine, you fought hard to keep it.

Having acquired H. Samuel, I wanted to buy Britain's other major high street jeweller, Ernest Jones. I thought it made good sense as they were pitched at the higher end of the market and sold Gucci and Cartier watches. With the three brands – Samuel's, Ratners, and Jones – I would own the entire market.

However, I was approached by Morgan Grenfell to see if I would be interested in buying the British branches of Zales, which was the world's biggest jeweller at the time. Zales was a huge American chain that had just been taken over by a Canadian outfit called the People's Jewellers. They had done an audit and decided to offload the UK arm. They had 90 branches nationwide that I could pick up for around £30 million, which was a small deal by the standards of the day. However, it was a tempting opportunity, so Morgan Grenfell arranged for a meeting with Marvin Zale who flew in especially from America.

Striking deals was all about power play in the Eighties – we were all trying to be J.R. Ewing – and so while I was talking strategy with my finance director Andrew Coppell and Roger Selig from Morgan Grenfell, we didn't worry too much about keeping Marvin waiting in reception. It was all part of our 'we don't really need you' negotiating position. After 20 minutes, we asked Roger's assistant to bring up our guest. He came back pale-faced with a message from the receptionist: Mr Zale had been kept waiting long enough and had left.

We later learned that he'd sold to Murray Gordon of Combined English Stores, the group that owned Salisbury's, the luggage shops, amongst other names. I felt I'd really missed out on something with the Zales deal, and having had a deal taken away from me, I wanted to come up with an even better deal. I was one of the most high-profile retailers at the time, and I knew the City would be pleased to see me move into other sectors, so I went to see Murray Gordon and suggested that we merged our companies. If I'm honest, I saw the 'merger' as an acquisition by another name – after all, my company was worth £400 million and his was only a £250 million business – but we agreed a deal that would mean I owned Zales, which is what I wanted. We announced the deal to the City and held a press conference, and our merger was widely hailed as an inspired move, but at the week-end there was a tiny piece in the *Sunday Times* that gave me cause for concern. It said that George Davies, the man behind Next, was planning a counter-bid for Combined English Stores.

When the markets opened on the Monday, I was told that Next had bought up 26% of CES stock on the open market. I then heard that they'd offered to buy the company for £300 million, which was £40 million more than I had valued the business at. I talked it over with Andrew and Roger, and we decided that we couldn't match it – which meant I had missed out on Zales for a second time.

I didn't like losing: I'd made up my mind I wanted Zales and it rankled that Next had bought it. I decided to give it one last go and made an appointment to see George Davies.

'I was never really interested in Combined English Stores', I told him. 'All I wanted was to get my hands on Zales.'

'You've been interested in it for some time from what I hear.'

'So it'll come as no surprise that I've come to make you an offer for it.'

'It better be a good one.'

I offered him £90 million for it, which was a ridiculous price, but as I keep saying, this was the Eighties and it paid to be flash. His eyes widened when he registered what I'd said: it was only making a profit of £6 or £7 million a year. He obviously thought he was on to a winner and decided it was too valuable to sell, which meant I had lost out on Zales for a third time.

Although I was annoyed, I wasn't as bothered as I might have been if I hadn't been quite a long way down the line in negotiations to buy Ernest Jones, which was a much bigger prize and a far more prestigious brand. Like H. Samuel, Ernest Jones was also a family business and the two sons of the founder, Ernest Weinstein (he'd changed the shop name to Jones because he thought Weinstein was too Jewish for British shoppers), were struggling to compete in a market dominated by the rampant Ratners group. Their shares had slumped and the company was valued at just £10 million. At that price, I wasn't the only one interested in them.

Ernest Weinstein had been a Major in the army and he was still known as 'Major Weinstein' in the business, partly because that's the way he ran his business. However, he was nearing 70 and was no longer the force he'd once been. His son Michael was now in charge and was fielding the offers from several suitors. One of them came from the man who was rapidly becoming my nemesis, George Davies. He had made them a good offer for the business, but Michael Weinstein was insisting that he and his brother Phillip had to remain on the board after any takeover. George Davies agreed they could sit on the board, but only if several stringent growth targets were met. It was clear that he had no intention of letting the Weinsteins have any say in their family company, and so they never signed the deal.

I, on the other hand, was happy to have one of them on the board. This wasn't enough, so I invented something I called the 'Management Board' that Phillip was asked to sit on. With only one of them on the Ratners main board they wouldn't have any real control, but creating a role for both of them was what they wanted. It convinced the Weinsteins that they would still be steering their company, and so they agreed to let Ratners buy Ernest Jones. I went to meet them at their headquarters, which was in a very nice building in Lisson Grove. I thought it was even lovelier when I learned that Ernest Jones owned the freehold and it would be part of the sale (a few years later I sold the building for £10 million, which made Ernest Jones an even better investment). We agreed the terms of the takeover and made an announcement to the City.

Despite our agreement, I didn't have an easy relationship with the Weinsteins. A few years later I would learn the hard way how it feels to have an outsider oust you from the family business, but at the time I don't think I understood what a painful move selling the company had been for the Weinsteins. Their sense of ownership over Ernest Jones inevitably led to clashes as I pushed to integrate their shops into my empire.

About three months after the takeover, we had a meeting of the Management Board. After the meeting, Michael and Phillip came up to me.

'We don't like the way you talked about our father in that meeting.'

'I'm sorry. I didn't mean to offend anyone, but it's clear he hadn't been running the company in the most sensible way.'

'You were incredibly rude.'

'It was unintentional, I… I…'

'I can't work with someone who insults my father', said Michael, 'so you've left me no choice but to resign'.

'You'll have my resignation on your desk tomorrow too', added Phillip.

I really can't remember what I had said that had upset them so much, but I think they must have been using my comments as an excuse: they realised they didn't really have a role to play in the enlarged company and probably saw no point in carrying on. I told them I was stunned, but that it seemed we couldn't work together, so I wouldn't try and persuade them to change their minds. On the one hand I was really quite pleased they had walked so soon, but on the other hand the integration process had barely begun and they had far too much knowledge in their heads about how things had been done and who to go to for certain pieces of information. They would have been useful if they'd stayed around for another six months.

There was a chance their departure would have a negative impact on morale in the Ernest Jones shops, so I arranged a meeting with most of the managers at the Lisson Grove HQ.

'As some of you now know', I began, 'Phillip and Michel Weinstein have decided to leave the company. I know many of you have worked with them for years and will join me in wishing them all the best in whatever they decide to do next.'

As I was talking, it was clear the staff hadn't come for small talk, so I cut short the speech I had planned and moved to reassure them that their jobs were safe and that nothing would change in the immediate future. After the reaction I'd had from H. Samuel managers, I had assumed that Ernest Jones managers would also respond well to the confidence I could inject into their flagging brand. I was wrong. One woman stood up and claimed to be speaking for a lot of people in the room. It became clear she had been very close to the Weinsteins.

'You wanted them to go from the start. Your behaviour has been disgusting and I cannot in all good conscience continue to work for you.'

'Is there anyone else who feels the same way?' I asked.

A few more hands went in the air. I'm not sure what the root of their resentment was, but I have a suspicion that they thought they were better than Ratners. Despite these hiccups, we were able to make changes at Ernest Jones that saw sales and profits increase, and when these things happen, staff morale isn't very far behind. Nevertheless, it was a tough couple of months.

I couldn't quite believe that Ratners now owned both H. Samuel *and* Ernest Jones. I was still a little annoyed that I had missed out on Zales, but felt a real sense of accomplishment to own the entire range of high street jewellers. The group now represented over 40% of all jewellery sales in the UK, and that gave us a lot of negotiating power with our suppliers. For instance, Ratners, H. Samuel and Ernest Jones all stocked Seiko watches, so I could go to them and say 'Right, I want a better deal'. I didn't need to threaten to stop stocking or promoting their product: they knew the clout we had, and so they would offer us incentives, like if we sold £30 million worth of watches, they'd give us a 2.5% retrospective discount. That instantly boosted our bottom line by £750,000, and when we did deals like that with all our suppliers, the profits we reported to the City leapt up each quarter.

There were also distribution benefits, as the same lorry could deliver to all three chains in a town on the same day, and of course there were other reductions in overheads, with centralised payroll and management. I assumed we could also get one area manager to cover all three chains and make a saving there too, but I quickly realised that was a mistake and reinstated area managers for each separate brand. That way they stayed competitive with each other, and when they were distinct from one another, the public responded to choice. Competition was good for the staff too: all the senior managers were on merit award schemes and stood to receive bonuses if sales reached certain targets.

In 1989 we were so confident we thought we could increase sales by 40%. This meant screaming our discounts from posters in our windows, but the public gets used to '50% off' posters and thinks it's a bit of a scam. So I devised an incentive scheme that grabbed their attention: spend £100 and get a £50 gift voucher free. The marketing side of the business had always been where I'd contributed the most, and using price to drive customers through the door was something I understood instinctively.

When I announced it, some of the managers – and a couple of the board members – thought I had gone mad and said such a move would bankrupt us. But I understood the shopper's mind, and I knew it would make money, not lose it. The psychology of such a voucher encourages people to spend £150 when they might otherwise have spent £120, so we were already £30 up; and when they came in to spend their voucher, they would often spend over the voucher amount. Because we sold our stock at a 50% mark up, we were only giving away £25 worth of stock, but as people were spending more per transaction, that cost was offset. To our bottom line, that £50 voucher was the equivalent of offering a 15% discount, but to the customer it was like getting a free gift and our sales kept on driving upwards. So we introduced a £100 voucher if you spent £300, and this had the same effect.

My job as chief executive really just came down to one thing: making sure this year's sales were significantly better than last year's, and once our stores were performing efficiently, the next best way to increase sales was to increase the number of shops. I was sure there was still a lot of room for growth in the jewellery market, and I thought again about expansion.

I wasn't the only one. George Davies had decided to use some of the stores he'd acquired in the Combined English Stores deal to open a new chain of jewellers. He had recently taken the Next brand successfully from apparel into home furnishings and believed his brand could be rolled out – a bit like the Virgin brand – to any number of ventures. In the late Eighties and early Nineties, he opened around 60 branches of Next Jewellers with the intention of being even higher end than Ernest

Jones. George Davies went to see suppliers like Rolex personally, as he knew if he could stock their watches it would be a clear indication to the public what kind of shop they were in.

A couple of my managers resigned to say that they had been offered a promotion and a pay rise with Next. That wasn't my only concern: while Ernest Jones was still performing weakly, I knew there was a chance that Next could do us some real damage at the top end of the market.

Rolex didn't play ball, however, and it seemed to me that Next had spent so much money making their shops look beautiful – they were a designer's dream – that they were going to have to shift a lot of stock to recoup their costs. Without the big names like Rolex, they were going to struggle to differentiate themselves from the competition. It soon became clear that the Next brand wasn't as transferable as George Davies had thought: the public saw it as a fashion brand, and many of them made the assumption that Next Jewellers must be selling costume and fashion jewellery. If you wanted real gold, and real gem stones, you were going to go to a proper jeweller who had been in the business for a long time. Consequently, the threat of Next was quite short-lived and some of the staff who had jumped ship phoned and asked if they could have their old jobs back. One of them had been quite senior in Next, so I asked John Hughes to make him an offer: he could have his old job back, with a pay rise, but only in six months' time. In the time being, he would act as our spy inside enemy territory. It was sneaky, but I think he quite enjoyed having a 'mission'.

The failure of Next Jewellers had a knock-on effect for the whole group. My spy told me that the group was very highly geared – i.e. their borrowing was too high in relation to their assets – and this was making the City very nervous. As their share price continued to fall, they spent millions of pounds trying to spend their way out of trouble.

So it wasn't a complete surprise when Roger Selig – who had brokered the Samuel deal when he'd been at Morgan Grenfell – approached me asking if I was still interested in buying Zales. I told him I was. Roger, who was now working independently, told me there was a catch: Next would only offload Zales as part of a package. If I wanted it, I would also have to buy Salisbury's, the luggage retailer. The combined price tag for both chains was £150 million. Even though it was a seriously inflated price and I didn't have any interest in selling handbags, I told Roger I'd buy both brands. That's how much I wanted Zales.

I went to meet George Davies to iron out the deal, and not surprisingly, he was much nicer to me than he had been a few years before. I was thrilled about the deal – owning Zales would take me to 50% of the UK jewellery market. So it was no wonder that the Monopolies and Mergers Commission wanted to investigate the sale. Initially Mr Hussein and Andrew Coppell handled all the contact with the Commission, but when things stalled, I arranged to visit the Head of the Commission at his office. He was concerned that I was already too dominant in the market, but as luck would have it, he lived in Bromley, and that just happened to be the only high street in Britain that didn't have a branch of H. Samuel. We only had a Ratners and an Ernest Jones there, and just by looking around his local shops he came to the conclusion that we weren't onerously dominant, and gave us the go-ahead on the Zales purchase. It was unbelievably lucky, and it's just another example of how things were going my way in those days. I suppose some people would say that my luck was bound to run out sooner or later.

We financed the deal largely through loans. It meant our gearing was at levels normally considered dangerous, but as our growth was so spectacular, the City was happy with our debt levels as our imminent growth would soon get our gearing within a healthy ratio to our assets. It was precisely this kind of confidence that stoked the market, and ultimately led to the crash in October 1987. When confirmation of the Monopolies and Mergers Commission's decision came into the office, I went berserk. I hadn't realised how much I had wanted Zales until I was told I had it. I'm sure it must have had something to do with the fact I'd missed out on it so many times before.

Shortly after we concluded the Zales deal, I got two other pieces of news that made me unbelievably happy. The first was the announcement that Next had taken the decision to shut down two large jewellery chains that it had acquired as part of the CES deal – Collingwood's and Weir's. In total, that removed 250 jewellers from the high street nationwide, which meant a large percentage of their customers would now find their way into one of my shops.

The other piece of good news was that British American Tobacco finally admitted defeat with their Jewellers' Guild shops and announced they were going to close all 40 of them down. The only competition I had now was from independent jewellers, and they would never be able to compete with me on price. There haven't been many retailers who have enjoyed such a dominant position in their chosen market.

While this gave me a massive opportunity to create efficiencies and drive down prices, there was a concern among some brokers in the City that Ratners was vulnerable: if there was a downturn in the jewellery market, then there weren't any other strings to my bow.

CHAPTER 14

The Incredible Eighties

Looking back, I can see that I was having fun, but I also remember that the business and its success wasn't making me happy at a fundamental level. Maybe I thought that if I just had a little bit more I'd be happy. Part of that 'little bit more' was getting a helicopter. It was such a ridiculous thing to have done, and I'm really a little embarrassed by it now, but in the Eighties everything was a bit over the top, and so I decided I would get a helicopter. I justified this to myself by saying that I spent a lot of my time visiting our shops round the country, and that if I got a phone call that meant I needed to be back in London very quickly, I wouldn't be able to make it. Somehow I convinced myself that having a helicopter would be *sensible*!

Ratners was making so much money at the time that Gary O'Brien, our new finance director who I'd brought in from Burtons, was actually looking for things to spend money on. Gary had replaced Andrew Coppell who – although he was a very personable and likeable Irish guy – had never really had the tenacity I'd wanted in an FD. If I ever asked Mr Hussein or John Hughes what the sales figures were in the Swindon branch, they would just tell me. Andrew would always have to look them up. Gary worked differently to Andrew and was very comfortable structuring complex deals and off-setting tax liabilities. If he told me I needed to spend money, then I was only too happy to oblige.

I went to visit Hanson's helicopter division to look at a few models. The first one they showed me was a little Squirrel, which was their cheapest model at $500,000 (for some reason, all helicopters were priced in dollars). Then they showed me a mid-range model, but I still wasn't all that impressed. So they let me climb aboard a Sikorsky 6-seater that cost $2.5 million. It was like being a rock star on a private plane. It had a separate passenger section with sound insulation so you didn't have to wear headphones, which meant you could have meetings in it. That was all the excuse I needed to justify getting my cheque book out. Getting money out of me in the Eighties was a bit like getting blood out of an artery.

When I got back to the office, Gary's eyes widened when I told him what I'd done.

'What kind of discount are they giving you?'

'Um, they said they would throw in some cushions.'

I really didn't care about the amount.

'Remind me to never let you negotiate the price of anything again!'

When I first saw it, I was more than a little embarrassed to see that Hanson's had put my initials on it: that was way too flash, even for me. Not only was the helicopter a waste of money, it was also a waste of time. Whenever I wanted to make a trip, the helicopter had to fly from its base in Blackbush to a helipad in Battersea. My driver then chauffeured me to the helipad, which in London traffic was never a quick journey. And then because travelling in a helicopter was so exciting, Victor and John Hughes wanted to come with me.

Victor found a field near his house in Stanmore where the helicopter could land, and John – who had moved to a big house in Kidderminster after I'd put him in charge of H. Samuel – built what I can only describe as an airport in his back garden. It was so typical of John: there wasn't anything he couldn't organise. It even had floodlighting so he could be picked up at night.

'I didn't buy a plane John, only a helicopter.'

I can only assume it impressed the neighbours, but once I'd picked up those two, a lot of the time it would have been quicker to take the train. Especially on the trips when we also picked up an area manager. Of course, at the end of the day when I just wanted to get home as quickly as possible, I had to drop them off on the way back to Battersea. On the up side, they both loved it and saw it as a real perk.

I started to get really annoyed with the helicopter when I went to visit our shops in Glasgow. The helipad Hanson used was at the airport.

'I could have got the plane and it would have been quicker', I said to the pilot. 'The whole point of a helicopter is that it can land where planes can't and that I can get straight to where I need to be.'

He explained that only the military and air ambulances could land anywhere: he needed a licence. The managers joked about painting an H on the roof of our shops – something I probably would have considered if it hadn't meant strengthening the entire buildings to take the weight. I often made the pilot land in places where he wasn't supposed to, and on one occasion the rotors hit a road sign and chopped it down. A week or so later, Lord Hanson himself phoned me to apologise.

'It won't happen again', he said, 'we have a rule that as soon as a pilot is involved in an accident then they are automatically asked to leave'.

'Actually, I think that would be a little unfair. It was really my fault, I made him land there.'

'That doesn't matter. He also breached our company rules.'

'But it's nearly Christmas. It really was my fault.'

In the end, the pilot kept his job and I learned that there was nothing I could safely do to make using the helicopter any quicker. The real benefit was that I could drop in on any shop without warning, and all the managers knew I could arrive at any time. When I turned up unannounced, they couldn't hide any problems from me, and this actually proved to be a very useful management tool: it meant I got to see the shops as they really were, which meant I saw them as the customers did. That perspective gave me ammunition when I was asking for changes or improvements.

A few years later, right at the end of the decade, I attended our AGM and one of our shareholders stood up and told me I had wasted shareholders' money on the helicopter. I defended my actions, explaining it helped me run the shops more efficiently.

'Well Anita Roddick doesn't visit all the branches of the Body Shop by helicopter, so I don't see why you need to.'

Looking back, I see her comments as part of a very delicate shift in the public's attitude. The Eighties had been called the 'Me Decade' and when the Nineties started, people started talking about the 'Caring Decade'. Owning a helicopter and flamboyant extravagance was starting to become unfashionable. However, I was so caught up in my own personal ambition that I wouldn't notice those changes for a few years yet.

A broker at one of our institutional investors, Standard Life, made similar comments.

'You're just building your company up for personal benefit now. Nothing you're spending money on is for the benefit of the shareholders.'

I told him I thought getting the share price up from 13p to £4.20 was for the benefit of shareholder investment, and that with those kinds of returns he had no right to question how I ran my business. He also told me he thought I had borrowed too much money to buy Zales, but I was in no mood to listen to a doom-monger. If I had, things may have been a little different a few years down the line.

In 1986, I ran the biggest jewellery retailer in Britain, I had a salary of £500,000 a year, and probably around £8 million worth of Ratners shares that paid another few hundred thousand a year in dividends. My wealth was considerable, but I was never in the same league as Branson or Sugar or other guys who still owned 50% of their companies.

My income brought me a very nice lifestyle – Moira and I flew on Concorde to stay at the Sandy Lane hotel in Barbados, or we'd charter a plane to take us skiing at Courcheval. If I had been bothered to collect the air miles, I might still be flying for free today, but saving money was not something that concerned me then.

The truth was I didn't really understand the value of what I had, not in personal terms, and therefore I didn't appreciate what I had beyond a few bragging points with Charles and Michael. That made me slightly uncomfortable: I knew I had things that other people didn't have, and I knew that many of them were frivolous. I look at it now like a 23-year-old Premiership footballer who goes out and buys a Bentley with his weekly pay packet. If he crashed it, he might not even bother to repair it, and I know for sure that he doesn't get nearly as much pleasure driving it as the 50-year-old who has saved for years to buy his Bentley. As I was to find out a few years later, one of the silver linings of losing everything is that you start to understand the value of possessions.

I'm not saying that money doesn't make you happy, but I do believe that only a certain amount of money makes you happy. Above a certain level you get into the realm of the law of diminishing returns. Buying more stuff doesn't make anyone happy in the long term.

However, this was still the Eighties, and that was a decade about accumulating as much stuff as you could get. Having made Ratners the biggest jeweller in Britain, I now resolved to make Ratners the biggest jeweller in the world. The big challenge for British retailers – the Holy Grail, in fact – was America. Lots of ambitious entrepreneurs had tried it, but they had all come back a few years later with their tails between their legs and their bank balances a few million pounds adrift – even Marks & Spencer had failed to crack America. So as well as expanding Ratners rapidly in the UK – we opened 150 shops in 1986 and 1987 – I saw America as the next logical challenge, and when a series of brokers told me that everybody would love me if I cracked the States, I knew that was exactly what I would try and do next. One chap at Morgan Grenfell added: 'However, if you squander a lot of investors' money on a dumb deal, the City will turn on you with venom.'

It's always hard to know exactly what drives someone in my situation: I had more money than I could ever spend, the ear of the most powerful politician for a generation, and my name illuminated on every high street in the country. The only explanation I have as to why I chose to continue to expand is ego. Like many other operators in the Eighties, I had an enormous ego. If I could make money in America, then my ego would be very happy.

CHAPTER 15

Going Global

Being the confident retailer that I was, the first company I approached was Tiffany's, the world's most glamorous jeweller. Although it's famous for its store on Fifth Avenue, it also has a worldwide operation, and there wasn't a bigger feather I could have put in my cap.

I flew to New York to meet the Tiffany's board. They were going through a rough patch and sales had started to slow, which is probably why they had agreed to meet me, but when they found out I wanted to buy them, I was told in no uncertain terms that Tiffany's was not for sale.

I had appointed two new firms of brokers – Cazenove and County NatWest – and both of them were relieved my overtures to Tiffany's had come to nothing. They had thought it was a bad fit with my existing shops, but when I told them I had also looked at another chain while I'd been in the States, they both told me I should pursue it.

The company was called Sterling, and they owned 125 shops around America trading under a variety of names. I had spotted them when a New York bank called Payne Webber took me on a tour of a suburban shopping mall in New Jersey. Unlike the UK where I had phoned up rival shops and tricked them into giving me their sales figures by pretending to be from 'head office', in America that information is available through the mall owners. I went to several malls, and in every one there were around eight jewellers, and the Sterling stores always had the highest figures.

I arranged a meeting with Sterling's owners at their headquarters in Akron, Ohio. Although I had been accused by some brokers of squandering shareholders' money, I didn't take an entourage with me on these trips – it was usually just Victor and me – and could change my plans at a moment's notice if a meeting was arranged. I liked the Sterling management team a lot, and this was something that made the company even more attractive. Even though failure wasn't in my vocabulary at the time, I wasn't arrogant enough to think that I could export the Ratners philosophy, and certainly not the Ratners brand. If I bought a company, I would also be buying the management, which was in complete contrast to the Samuel and Ernest Jones takeovers.

I felt the reason other British retailers had failed was because they had tried to impose a British business, and a British style of doing business, on the American market. I knew I hadn't spent enough time there to understand the market, so I wasn't looking for something I could turnaround: I was looking for a success story I could watch expand, and Sterling fitted the bill perfectly. In my eyes, it didn't really matter what I paid for it, as long as I was buying a sound business. On the same trip I passed on the chance to buy an LA chain called Barry's. It was in trouble and on offer at a knockdown price, but I knew I didn't have the market knowledge to turn it around. It was a great investment for someone else, but I was sure it was the wrong company for me.

When news that I had offered Sterling's president, a man with the rather fabulous name of Nate Lite, £125 million for his company reached the *Financial Times* in London, they reported that I had made the offer with 'indecent haste'. They weren't wrong, as the company was probably only worth about £40 million. I made it clear to Nate that I didn't want to miss out on what I saw as a terrific opportunity, and so he had named his price and agreed to become my employee. I really didn't care about the price, but there was just one part of the deal that made me flinch: as salaries in the States were so huge, I was going to have to quickly get used to the fact that I would have an employee who earnt about three times as much as me. Call me traditional, but isn't the boss supposed to earn the most?

I discussed my finance options with David Mayhew at Cazenove, and decided that the best way to pay for the deal was through a share issue. However, I was already in the middle of a share issue to raise £150 million to finance my expansion in the UK and the City wouldn't like another one so soon afterwards. David, who you would expect to be very conservative about these matters, simply said: 'Well let's cancel the first share issue and announce a new one and we'll raise all the money in one go.' It's the kind of move investors wouldn't appreciate any more, but in 1986 the stock market was still rising steeply and it felt like it would go on rising for ever.

I was fascinated by the differences between the jewellery business in the UK and the US business. The American public bought jewellery in a totally different way. For instance, they wouldn't buy a diamond unless they had looked at it through a gemscope, and when they did buy it they always bought it on in-store credit. Sterling was making a huge proportion of its profits from its financing arrangements. I was stunned at the average ticket price of Sterling's goods. Most of our rings sold around the £300 mark, but the American shops' most popular item was a $3500 one-carat diamond ring. And those high ticket prices meant they made phenomenal margins on every sale, sometimes over 60%, compared with Ratners' 52%. They didn't even bother to restock their best-selling lines: if something went out of stock and became unavailable, that only made it more desirable to American shoppers. The fact that there wasn't a unifying brand name on all the shop fronts was also different: in Britain, customers trusted a national brand; in America, they wanted to believe they were buying something unique from a boutique retailer.

I was also surprised to learn that American jewellers spent a lot of money – perhaps 7% of their turnover – on advertising, something that I had found out to my cost a few years earlier made next to no difference in the UK. I had been in the jewellery trade for 22 years when I did the Sterling deal, and I was amazed that it counted for nothing: there wasn't a single thing I could teach them. Of course, I didn't tell the City that: they heard that my expertise would see Sterling's profits soar and that it was a marriage made in heaven.

However, there was one crucial way in which Sterling was like Ratners, and that was why I was confident in paying so much for it. Sterling had a formula that worked, and like Ratners, it could be quickly replicated. I wanted to get to a thousand shops in America, and Sterling gave me the blueprint to do that. I felt I could take it from a 4% share to a 20% share of the US market in little more than a couple of years, and so I set Nate on the acquisition trail. Some analysts might have thought I overpaid, but I knew I had struck a very good deal.

I spent remarkably little time in the States after the initial deal was concluded, but Nate and I spoke on the phone regularly as he bought a chain of 80 shops here, and 100 shops there. The first couple of deals were funded by a straightforward rights issue, helped by our dual listing on both the London and New York stock exchanges. As the deals continued, the brokers advised us that investors thought we were creating too many shares, and so to make each issue more attractive, Gary O'Brien devised increasingly complicated ways of structuring deals. We used every instrument available to us – convertible shares, preference shares – and it was so complicated that I barely understood it. What I did understand, however, is that whatever we called the mechanism we used, it was really just another way of taking on more debt. If we weren't careful, our gearing could reach uncomfortable levels.

Within two years, our American operation had expanded from the original 125 shops to 500. The Americans love rapid expansion, and so we got a lot of attention and goodwill from American investors. However, the entire global economy was about to hit the buffers, and not even a rampant Ratners would be immune from the fallout.

I remember taking a group of investors and analysts round the Mondales warehouse, which we had moved to a massive new building in Edgware Road, the week before the stock market crash. Inside the warehouse we had built replicas of Ratners, Ernest Jones and

H. Samuel shops to show how the merchandise would be displayed on the high street. At the end of my presentation, they all seemed very impressed and started asking questions about my father's photo system and other distribution matters. Then a guy called Paul Deacon from Goldman Sachs stood up and asked:

'Is there anything that can go wrong?'

I made up some waffle and talked about how a Labour government had once brought in a high rate of luxury tax on jewellery, but apart from something like that – completely out of our control – I had to say, no, I couldn't see that anything could go wrong. This was on Friday 16th October. On Monday 19th, the stock market crashed and a few of those analysts sent me jokey messages reminding me of what I had said.

Ratners shares went from £4.20 to £2.10 in the space of three days. As I didn't have a huge amount of shares, I wasn't too bothered: I was more concerned that the business was in good shape, and compared with many businesses I could see floundering around me, I was very confident about Ratners' prospects. It's impossible in a crash to be immune, but I felt we hadn't taken the hit some others had.

The crash had cut a little deeper on Wall Street than it did in the City, and so companies with American interests found their share prices stayed low. This made me a little depressed until Nate came over to visit. We went to look at some of our stores, and while we were walking round Brent Cross shopping centre in North London, he said to me: 'People here are not talking about the stock market: it doesn't affect them so they are still buying stuff.'

I looked at him and he was smiling: I knew he was right, but in the weeks after the crash I had spent so much of my time talking to investors and analysts that the share price had started to consume my every waking thought. For just about the only time in my career, I had forgotten about the customer. I considered myself very lucky to realise that the customer hadn't forgotten about Ratners.

'You're right', I said, 'We're doing absolutely fine'.

There had been talk for months that shares were over-valued, but just as people today talk about house prices being too high, the price inflation had gone on for so long that many of us had started to think that a crash would never happen: if there was a 'correction', few of us believed it would be that severe.

Somebody once said to me that the stock market always tells you the truth, that a share price can't lie. But I didn't believe that: I knew our business was robust, and that customers were still buying our products. Few Britons owned shares, so the wider economy wasn't affected: consumer confidence was the lever that kept my business booming. What I should have realised, perhaps, is that eventually the stock market crash would filter through to the jobs market and into interest rate rises, and that one way or the other, a recession was looming. But from where I was sitting at the end of the Eighties, the future looked rosy, so I started searching around for our next acquisition.

On the home front, I was aware that I no longer had a personal investment in property. House prices were doubling every couple of years at the time and although I enjoyed living in the house in Arlington Street, I was aware it wasn't really home. It was right in the middle of Piccadilly and didn't have a garden, but more importantly, it was a company asset, not a personal one. As I had no reason to think that I would ever have to leave it (which was very optimistic of me, considering what happened in the Nineties), it made sense to buy outside of London. One day in 1989, I went for a drive and found myself walking along the Thames near Bray in Berkshire. I looked enviously at all the houses with river views, and when I saw that one of them was for sale, I decided to buy it. Even though it cost £1.7 million.

I had anticipated buying something around the £900,000 to £1 million mark, but I justified the price tag of this house (a) because it was a beautiful white weather boarded New England style house and (b) because it had a plot of land next to it that I thought I could sell for £800,000. I needed to get a mortgage for it, but with my salary, the repayments wouldn't be a problem. Nor would the renovations budget, which added another couple of hundred thousand to the price. My idea was that it would be the perfect place for Suzy and Lisa to come and spend the weekends with me.

I was still technically married to Angela at this point. We had deliberately taken the slow route to our Decree Absolute because we both found the idea of divorce so final. We didn't want it, but we agreed it was an inevitability and hoped we would both be able to move on from it. Moira – who had stopped working for me as we recognised that working with each other as well as dating each other would sooner or later affect our relationship either at home or at work – was very understanding of our situation and didn't put any pressure on me to speed things along. She was still in her twenties, and probably too young to think seriously about a future with me anyway.

That was about to change, however, when she told me she was pregnant. Just a couple of weeks later, I took a phone call from Angela who was about to sign the final pieces of paperwork that would end our marriage.

'I'm not sure I can do it Gerald. I wonder if we should try again, for the sake of the girls if not for ourselves.'

If she had said this to me a couple of years beforehand I would almost certainly have said 'yes', but when I told her Moira was pregnant, she knew the decision we'd avoided making for several years had finally been made for us. Our divorce was finalised a couple of weeks later.

CHAPTER 16

Riding the Acquisitions Express

Ratners had 50% of the UK jewellery market and was reaching saturation point, so I knew if I wanted a big deal to continue to grow the business it would come from America. I didn't much enjoy the trips to visit the Sterling HQ. Akron is the epitome of Hicksville, and although Nate had moved to some nice offices, the only other thing I could recommend about the place was the breakfasts. Mr Hussein, on the other hand, loved America, and our colleagues out there loved him, so he started to spend a lot of time there. Although I managed to avoid making too many trips, when Nate phoned me up and told me there was a really big deal on the table, I got on the next plane I could.

Gordons owned a chain of 600 shops, compared with the 500 Sterling was now operating. They weren't performing very well, and were a target for a takeover. Zales – the massive US jeweller whose UK shops I had tortuously acquired a couple of years previously – were also interested and we learned that they had already bid $40 a share for Gordons, which valued them at around $500 million. So we offered them $42 a share, and they accepted. All I had to do now, I thought, was raise the money.

The obvious way to do it was through another share issue, but when I suggested this at the next board meeting, I encountered unexpected opposition. Terry Jordan, who was on the verge of retirement, had long been the single biggest shareholder since I'd bought his company in 1984. He was very concerned about 'shareholder value', something that had never been the top of my list of concerns. He was, rightly, worried that another share issue would see the share price deflate – and his retirement fund slashed at a stroke.

It would have been easy to dismiss his hostility to the Gordons deal as self-interest, but Victor was also against it. I got the impression that Victor's nose had been put out of joint by the shift in emphasis away from the UK and towards the US operation, where he wasn't involved at all. It was almost as if Nate had replaced him as the company's golden boy and I sensed a personal rivalry between them. This made me wonder if I could rely on Victor's objections, so we turned to an analyst called John Richards for his opinion. I've never forgotten his reply. After careful consideration, he though the acquisition would cause 'some indigestion': the shares would probably dip by 20 or 30 pence, but once the Gordons stores were converted to Sterling stores and their profits increased, then our share price should recover.

Only Mr Hussein shared my enthusiasm for the purchase, so we decided to ask an outsider's opinion. Victor, Terry, Mr Hussein, Andrew Coppell, and I all walked into my office where I called Michael Green.

'Hi Michael.'

'Hi Gerald.'

'We've got a little bit of a disagreement this end, and I'd like to know what you think.'

I had often used Michael and Charles as unofficial non-executive board members round the snooker table, and I knew he understood my business almost as well as I understood his. He listened carefully: we also had the option of taking out a loan for the purchase, and the bank had already indicated that they would write out a cheque if we asked, but that would take our gearing to dangerous levels, especially as we could see the very early indicators of a recession around us.

Michael's advice was very pertinent: 'You can be unpopular with the press, that doesn't really matter; you can be unpopular with the City, all that will happen is that your shares go down; but the people you don't want to be unpopular with is the banks: if there's a chance you won't be able to repay the loans, then you shouldn't do it.'

We carried on talking after I'd put the phone down on Michael, and we eventually came to the decision not to proceed. I was on the brink of 40, and I had clearly mellowed a bit. I guess I thought they were right: perhaps I had been a bit mad on acquisitions for the past couple of years. The younger me would have bulldozed ahead no matter what, but it was unusual for so many of the team to question me that I suppose I began to question myself. I bottled it, basically, and of course Zales snapped Gordons up and it turned out to be an incredibly lucrative deal for them. I really felt I had let one of the big prizes of my career slip through my fingers, and I was furious.

I went home to the house in Bray and was almost inconsolable. It didn't help when Mr Hussein phoned to let me know that he thought we'd made a big mistake.

'I think we have destroyed our future', I remember him saying.

Over the next months and years, we watched Zales make a success of Gordons, and I never really stopped kicking myself.

Towards the end of 1989, we started to notice the recession begin to bite in America. Sales were slightly down in the Sterling shops (although they took between $1 and $2 million each a year), and I was still interested in another US acquisition. Kays was one of the biggest chains in the country, owning over 500 jewellery stores, mostly on the West Coast. If I could buy Kays I would have a thousand shops in America to match the thousand I had in the UK. When their share price dropped to a level that I thought was seriously under-valued, Nate and I discussed a takeover.

I felt personally under pressure to deliver continued growth. The brokers' forecasts for 1989 were that Ratners would make a £65 million profit (by 1992 that forecast would leap to £220 million), and despite the fact that it was only five years since we'd been posting profits of £1 million, I would come in for criticism if I didn't deliver on their forecasts. I saw buying Kays as a way of buying profits, and so I approached its CEO. Not enough of their shares were available on the open market to get any leverage, so I needed him to agree to a takeover. Unfortunately for me, he turned me down. When I got back to London I asked Mr Hussein to stay on top of Kays' position: if anything changed, I was prepared to move on it again.

Having missed out on Gordons and Kays, I decided to buy myself a consolation present. And as I never had a modest ambition in those days, I thought I might like to buy myself a major high street brand – Dixons. The brokers were demanding growth – they were used to me doubling my profits each year – and if that growth wasn't going to come from the jewellery sector, then Ratners needed to diversify into other areas. I didn't have some grand plan to strategically expand into certain activities, I was simply opportunistic, and Dixons represented a massive opportunity.

I had always admired Dixons as a business, and had been quoted many times saying so in the press. Their growth in recent years had been exceptional, and growth was what I needed. I knew that if I was able to get hold of it, then I would be securing a practically guaranteed way of meeting the brokers' targets.

I'd been prompted into making an approach because Dixons had become a target for the Kingfisher group, which owned B&Q and Woolworth's. If it got sucked up by such a big company, I knew I would never get the chance to own it again. Of course, I couldn't really afford Dixons, but I thought my old trick of 'let's try a merger' might see me get control of it without having to pay too much for it.

I went to see Stanley Kalms, who was the chairman, and told him how much I admired his business, especially now that Tony Dignum had returned to the company where he had done so much good before his move to H. Samuel. Stanley was nearly 60, and it seemed suitable that he should become chairman of the merged company, and I would be chief executive. He liked the idea enough – it was preferable to being consumed by Kingfisher – to invite me to meet Dixons' directors at their next board meeting.

I went with Andrew Coppell, and we talked over how a merger might work. We all felt we could work together, and began detailing who would do what in the combined company. Once we had agreed a plan, we had to convince the City it was the best move for both companies. The Kingfisher bid had been referred to the Monopolies and Mergers Commission because they also owned Currys, so that bought Stanley and me a bit of time to persuade the big institutional investors to support the merger.

I needed to raise around £800 million for the deal, and I got Global Electra – one of the big pension funds – to promise £50 million if I could raise the rest. This was a great start, so when I went to see the other big institutional investors – Warburgs, the Prudential – I was confident of piecing together a deal. But one by one they all turned me down. It was such a big deal that they had to be 100% sure of the merged company's success. They had teams of people analysing every bit of retail data in existence, and the data was starting to show the beginnings of a downturn. I began to doubt if I would be able to raise the money.

Meanwhile, Mr Hussein was still trying to buy Kays. By this stage we had finally moved to plush new offices in Stratton Street, and we would pass each other on the stairs and say 'How's your deal going?'

'Not so well. The pension people are worried. How about Kays?'

'Actually, I think I may have found a way.'

Encouraging news from America was all I needed to go cold on the Dixons deal, so we sat down and started talking about how we might make it happen. I think I had only recently started to appreciate just what a huge asset Mr Hussein had been to the company. At times I had found him a bit obsequious – although his ability to suck up to people meant he had been brilliant as go-between for my father and grandfather 20 years before – but I was starting to realise that he cared about the company in just the same way as my family did. When I had first taken over the company, I had occasionally over-ruled him on decisions because he hadn't worked in our shops and didn't know how things worked at the coal face. Yet if it hadn't been for him and some very astute accounting, not to mention his ability to work around my father, Ratners could have gone bust on a number of occasions. He'd held the firm together with sticky tape and bits of string and he had been there so long that people went to him for information and solutions to problems. He was so deeply embedded in the company that I couldn't have got rid of him, even if I'd wanted to, which I didn't.

In many ways he was like Jack: you could shout and scream at him and be convinced you'd won the argument, but he would just go away quietly and do what he had planned to do anyway. I had also used him over the years to do some dirty jobs – like making several of the Salisbury's staff redundant when we tried to streamline that operation – and he fully deserved to be a director of the company. At the beginning he'd been paid peanuts, but by the end of the Eighties he was on £400,000 a year and had stock options worth a couple of million. It was nice to know his loyalty had been rewarded, and now he was going to be instrumental in securing a deal that would dramatically increase the size of the company.

Mr Hussein had established that the Dutch owner of Kays, Anthonie Van Ekris, could be persuaded to sell if we paid him a fee that compensated him for a non-compete agreement he would have to sign when the deal was concluded. That fee was £5 million: it seemed like a small price to pay.

Gary raised the $500 million we needed through another of his complicated share issues. Investors were concerned, quite rightly, that the recession was depressing consumer confidence in America and our profits per store were starting to dip. The concern was that if the share price dipped and our market capitalisation was downgraded, then our debt would be too high in relation to our net worth. The optimum level for gearing would have been around 30 or 40%, but if our share price dropped, Gary's latest share issue could see our gearing rise to 50 or 60%. That makes a company very vulnerable and encourages shareholders to bail out. When we announced the deal to the City, some commentators wondered if we'd done a deal too far.

I was still bullish, however, and knew that Nate would quickly impose the Sterling formula on the Kays stores and our turnover would shoot up. I felt Ratners could do no wrong and we outperformed our sector so spectacularly that it was as if we could walk on water. Our aim with the Kays stores was to increase each shop's annual turnover from £1.2 million to £2 million, a slightly more modest increase than we'd managed with some of our other US takeovers. Our financial director in America, a guy named Dick Miller, told me we wouldn't be able to do it. Previously, Dick had been as bullish as me, and I knew when he said it that we had probably overpaid for Kays. Still, we wouldn't lose on the deal, and I was still confident we'd outsell the competition. The key fact remains that my decision to go to the States was one of the best things that ever happened to Ratners. Perhaps not every decision was right, but my strategy of using local management was spot on. Nate continued to run the US division for many years, and today it's run by his son and their 1200 shops make $200 million a year.

The Kays deal meant I could claim to be the world's biggest jeweller with 2000 shops on two continents. I put that claim in our annual report, but no one gave a damn about it except me: they just wanted to know about earnings per share and forecasts for the next year. But for me, being the world's biggest jeweller meant something. It had been a long-held ambition, and I had achieved it.

To put it simply, life was good in 1989. In April, Moira had given birth to our daughter Sarah, and that summer we had married. It was a very small registry office ceremony with only family invited. Michael Green came, but only because I had bumped into him the day before and he'd asked what I was doing at the weekend. 'Getting married', I'd said casually. I'd been married before, and I just didn't want to make the same sort of fuss again.

In the 20 or so years since my first wedding, my parents' views on 'marrying out' had softened. I don't think they even mentioned the fact that Moira wasn't Jewish, or that our daughter would not be raised in the faith. If there was a hint of disapproval at our marriage, it came from Nigel Dempster, who wrote about our wedding in his column in the *Daily Mail*. He thought it was something of a scandal that our daughter was at the wedding. His disapproval seems very anachronistic now.

We moved from the house in Arlington Street to a bigger place with a lovely conservatory in Balfour Mews. It was another company purchase, but as it was one I had chosen, it felt a lot more like home and a lot less like an office. As I stood on the threshold of a new decade, I thought I had it all to look forward to. I was wrong.

ACT II
The Fall

CHAPTER 17

Welcome to the Nineties

Financially, the Nineties didn't get off to a great start. At the end of 1989 I had turned down an offer of £750,000 for the piece of land next to my home in Bray as I thought I could get a bit more for it. By the middle of 1990 I couldn't shift it. The impact of the stock market crash from 1987 had finally filtered through to the housing market, and with City bonuses slashed for the third year in a row due to the subdued performance of shares, the market for luxury houses in London's stockbroker belt had all but disappeared.

Added to that, the house I had bought for £1.7 million and spent hundreds of thousands of pounds on was losing value every week. To make matters worse, interest rates were rising steeply to cope with the high inflation caused by the consumer boom of the Eighties. At one point, my mortgage repayments were £19,000 a month. Even with my salary, that was the kind of expenditure that puts a dent in your lifestyle.

As my house was on the river, I'd obviously bought a boat that I didn't need and moored it at the end of the garden. Because that's what you did in the Eighties. Of course I never used it, and that was starting to be the kind of outlay I could no longer justify. I still had a terrific salary – £650,000 or so – and the perks of company expenses, but my shares had halved in value and I was starting to feel the squeeze.

Yet Ratners seemed, by and large, to be immune from the wider economic downturn. By 1991, Next's share price had collapsed to 6p, Marks & Spencer was on the slide, and we were one of the very few retailers defying the recession. This brought us a lot of attention, especially as it's usually the luxury goods retailers that suffer most in a slump: people will always need milk, but they can do without a new pair of earrings. Commentators were amazed at our continuing rise in profits, and I was personally credited with making the company a success.

Consequently, I started getting a lot of invites to do after-dinner speaking so I could explain how we'd bucked so many trends. I was nervous at first, but soon found that if the audience laughed at my first joke, I grew in confidence and fairly quickly became quite good at it. I also enjoyed it, but each time I stood up to give a speech, I was undermined by a little bit of doubt. Why hadn't we suffered as other companies had? It was almost as if I was standing on a roof waiting to jump. Everyone knew we couldn't keep it up for ever, and I had a sense people were waiting for me to fail.

It was around this time that I took Moira, our baby Sarah and my eldest daughter Suzy on holiday to America. The idea was that they could do some shopping and lie on a Florida beach while I had a couple of meetings with Nate Lite. The trip was reasonably uneventful, but on the flight home I came as close to death as I had since the day when I'd been struck by lightning in my pram.

Our plane was not long out of Miami when the cabin, very suddenly, filled with smoke. It wasn't like smoke from a bonfire, it was so thick that you couldn't see your hand if you held it right in front of your face. You couldn't even see the oxygen masks that had dropped down, but the cabin crew screamed at us to put them on and so we reached out blindly until we found them.

My first thoughts were for my wife and children. I held their hands, even though I couldn't see them, and talked to them and told them how much I loved them. The crew and the captain kept telling us that we would be all right, and so I kept repeating this to Moira and

Suzy. I was as scared as I have ever been, but it had all happened so quickly that I don't think I had time to think that we were all about to die.

The pilot announced that we were diverting to the Bahamas and that we would be on the ground within 15 minutes. I don't know if he said that to calm us, but it felt a lot longer to me, and as the plane dropped dramatically to get us on the ground as soon as possible, every minute felt like our last.

When we landed, I think my heart actually stopped beating. I was completely frozen as I just waited to be told it was over. As soon as we hit the ground, people started cheering inside their masks, and when the doors were opened and we could take them off, the sense of relief was incredible. Suzy was so traumatised that she had to be given Valium to calm her down. I felt simultaneously weak and elated, and it was wonderful just to be alive.

However, that was by no means the worst thing that happened to me in the early Nineties. In January 1991, my mother finally succumbed to the cancer she had fought for over 30 years. My father had remained devoted to her to the end, and my fear was for his mental health as he faced life without her in the months that followed.

When someone has fought cancer for so long, there is a feeling that they will somehow continue to fight it for ever, so her passing came as a shock. At the same time, when someone has suffered so much over so many years, there is also a sense of relief that the suffering has come to an end.

She had lived long enough to know that Moira was pregnant again. Like me, she secretly hoped the new baby would be a boy, and on the day she died, Moira called from the hospital to say that a scan had shown we were expecting a son. Jonathan was born the following August, and my delight at his arrival was immense.

My mother had been such a huge force in the business for so many years that many of the employees had met her at some point. I was inundated with condolence cards and good wishes. One of the cards came from Terry Jordan's second wife. She had become friendly with my mother – they had met when my mother had shopped in a dressmaker's where Terry's wife worked – and she wrote that my mother had told her how proud she was of me. There are few emotions to beat the knowledge that you have made your parents proud.

CHAPTER 18

An Invitation

Much as I missed my mother, in the months that followed her death there were several occasions when I was grateful that she did not live to see my downfall. It had started a few months earlier with a phone call from the Institute of Directors – a very influential association of some of the leading lights of the economy – asking me to give a keynote speech at their annual conference at the Royal Albert Hall. Two of the other scheduled speakers were the then Chancellor John Major and former South African President F.W. de Klerk (although by the time of the event, Major would have become Prime Minister and his replacement at the Treasury, Norman Lamont, took his place). This was an invitation as prestigious as a private lunch with Margaret Thatcher, and not only would I be speaking in front of 4000 of the most influential people in public life in Britain, but the event would be recorded for future television broadcast. I was incredibly flattered to have been asked, and so of course I said yes.

I had been making presentations to brokers and analysts for six or seven years by this point, and had always been complimented on my delivery. I had a reputation for plain speaking and avoiding the kind of jargon that can send audiences to sleep. I also never really cared about making myself seem big or clever, and many of my jokes were at my own expense. Once, at a speech I gave at the Café Royal, I followed my broker John Richard onto the podium on which he'd said

'50 per cent off' posters were a waste of time because you should be trying to build a loyal customer base. I stood up and said I disagreed: 'I'll take money from anyone!' This was not the kind of comment chairmen of major PLCs made; it went down well and comments like that earned me a reputation for having the common touch. I was a good foil to boring analysts and advisers in pinstriped suits and was often added to the bill as a bit of light entertainment. The more successful Ratners became, the more eager the audiences were and the more they responded. By the time of the IOD speech, I had a reputation that meant I'd already won the audience over by the time I stood up.

Shortly after I had accepted the invitation to speak, I called up Lynne Franks who had one of the best reputations in PR at the time (she was later said to be the inspiration for Jennifer Saunders' character in *Absolutely Fabulous*). I knew the IOD speech was a chance to create a public image, and I wanted her advice. She listened to what I had to say about the state of the business and the plans we had for the future. She looked at some of the speeches I had given in the past, and then she said something very profound.

'You know Gerald, I think you should forget about all of that. It's all a bit, um, well it's a bit Eighties if I'm honest. I think you need to sell yourself as a new breed of chief executive and present a vision that's more in keeping with the times.'

'I'm not sure I really know what you mean. It's the Institute of Directors I'm speaking to.'

'I know, but I think you should tear this up and write a speech about doing business ethically.'

'Like Anita Roddick?'

'A bit like that, yes. It's a new decade, there's a new spirit out there – people are becoming greener, more ecological. I think you have an opportunity here to put yourself at the head of a new movement.'

I thought she was being very hippyish about the whole thing, and completely ignored everything she had said. I decided I would carry on refining the speech I had given several times before. When the time came, the organisers of the IOD conference told me the system was set up for speakers to use autocue. This wasn't something I'd tried before – I'd always talked from notes – and it meant I had to send them a copy of my speech in advance so it could be typed into the system. It was clear this was a speech that would be taken seriously, so I actually called a consultancy run by the MP, now Lord, Greville Janner that advised people on public speaking. Greville came to see me in my office and I showed him the speech I'd written. I had given a version of the speech several times before, but as the IOD was such an esteemed institution, I'd left out some of the jokes. One gag that had always got a laugh was a comment about how H. Samuel was able to sell a sherry decanter for less than a tenner (punch line: because it was total crap); I'd also ditched another joke about a pair of our earrings that were cheaper than a Marks & Spencer prawn sandwich.

He looked it over and suggested places where I should put more emphasis or where I needed to pause. It wasn't advice worth paying for, but at least it made me confident the speech would go down well. As well as Greville, the IOD also sent over their public speaking adviser to train me. I was starting to understand just what a big deal addressing the IOD really was.

As it was such a high-profile speech, I'd also sent copies to Ratners' directors for their thoughts and input. John Gilham, the one director who had survived from H. Samuel, read and approved it. Then I showed it to Gary O'Brien and Mr Hussein. Gary came into my office carrying a copy of it, but was too interested in the gossip I'd got from having dinner with Asil Nadir the night before. We got so wrapped up in talking about Asil's belief that Polly Peck shares were about to soar after the scandal that had seen the value of his company – which owned everything from electronics manufacturers to fresh fruit producers – plummet in the previous months, that we never got round to discussing my speech. I could only conclude it met with his approval.

Mr Hussein, who was always methodical, came to see me, and he had read it carefully. He'd been to see me give speeches on several occasions, and I valued his opinion.

'I think you should put in a couple of jokes. People like your jokes.'

'Well the one that always goes down well is the one about the prawn sandwich lasting longer than our earrings.'

'Yes, put that one in.'

I'd originally made a version of the joke at a presentation to City analysts at which a couple of financial journalists were present. I had been trying to make the point about how cheap jewellery was getting with new production methods. 'It's fantastic for the public', I said. 'We can now make a pair of gold earrings for 99p. That's less than Marks and Spencer charge for a prawn sandwich. And they'll last a lot longer.' Maggie Urry from the *Financial Times* then said under her breath: 'You mean the sandwich will last a lot longer.' When this got a big laugh, the next time I told the story, I changed the punch line.

Maggie was also partly responsible for the other joke that brought me so much trouble. Back in 1986, she had been following me and Victor around for a couple of days as she was profiling us for a feature she was writing for the *FT* on management teams. We'd taken her to our warehouse to show her some of our merchandise and procedures. I told her I was surprised how well H. Samuel was doing with its gift merchandise. I'd gone on the record many times saying I didn't see the point of stocking larger gift items when that space could be given over to smaller and more expensive items of jewellery.

'Look at this' I said, holding up a sherry decanter. 'We sell this with six glasses on a silver-plated tray in a presentation box for £9.95.'

She looked perplexed: 'How can you sell it for such a price?'

'Because it's crap!' I said off the cuff. Anyway, she laughed, Victor laughed, the warehouse manager laughed, and it became one of my stock jokes. She put it in her piece for the *FT*, and it became quite a well-known joke within the City. That year, Goldman Sachs even awarded one of those sherry decanters to their top salesman at their annual dinner. A year later, when I was becoming very high profile, the *Sun* wrote a nice piece about me saying how my sense of humour made a breath of fresh air in the City. They ran a little sidebar next to the piece with the heading 'Gerald's gems'. In it they listed some of my jokes – and both the prawn sandwich joke and the crap comment were in there.

As I was amending my speech by hand, with Mr Hussein still sitting in my office, I became confident these jokes would go down as well with the IOD audience as they had with everyone else for the past four or five years. As I scribbled over the manuscript, I read out loud as I wrote... *H. Samuel sells a sherry decanter...* Mr Hussein stopped me.

'Don't say H. Samuel', he suggested. 'Just say Ratners. It's coming from you, and that sounds better.'

Ratners sells a sherry decanter... I scrawled, completely unaware of the consequences of my actions. I posted the amended speech to the IOD, but forgot to send the new version to the rest of the directors.

A couple of days before I was due to give the speech, the PR agency handling publicity for the event called and said that they had given copies of the speech to the press and there'd been a bit of interest, mainly from the *Daily Mirror* who would be sending a journalist to cover the event.

'That's great', I said.

Of course, what the PR should have said was that the *Mirror* was sending a lynch mob, but I'm getting ahead of myself. In the run up to the speech, there were a couple of incidents that might, with hindsight, have been clues that the speech wasn't going to have quite the impact I had imagined.

The first was at the rehearsal at the Albert Hall. The IOD's public speaking adviser was there, letting me know when to speak up, and when to pause in anticipation of applause. The girl monitoring the autocue called him over for a moment, then he shouted up to me.

'This girl's just spotted the word "crap". Is that right? Is it meant to say crap?'

'Um, yes. That's right.' I suddenly felt embarrassed by it. Maybe it was the wrong thing to say at the IOD after all.

The second thing that should have made me pause for thought was a lunch I had arranged with David Brewerton. He had been the *Telegraph* journalist who had written the original piece raising the idea that Ratners should buy H. Samuel. He had since left journalism and moved into PR, and he worked for one of the big City agencies called Brunswick PR. He wanted Ratners to switch agencies and start using Brunswick, so he had invited me out to lunch. He was free the day before the speech.

'That'll be perfect', I said, 'I can run through the speech with you and you can give me some free advice'.

David cancelled lunch at the last minute. No one had cancelled lunch on me for nearly 10 years. I was really taken aback, especially as he was trying to sell me something. I now wonder if his contacts on the newspapers had tipped him off about a story they were planning and he just didn't know if he would be able to look me in the eye.

This didn't help to settle my nerves, so I decided to take the IOD's advice and take things easy. I went home early and invited Michael Green round for a drink. He took a look at the manuscript, and didn't make any comments about a certain four-letter word. Michael is actually surprisingly conservative about these things, and if he wasn't bothered by it, then I was sure no one else would be. Just the previous week, I had made the crap joke at a lunch attended by Princess Anne. If I could say 'crap' in front of royalty, then it would be fine for a bunch of chief executives and economists. Only Moira questioned if it was right. 'It's just not that sort of event', she said.

In the morning of the event, my dad came round. He was very proud that I was making the speech and wanted to come to the Albert Hall with me. He'd never heard me do any public speaking before, so I knew that him putting a suit on and making the effort meant he thought addressing the IOD was a very big deal.

He came in the limousine with me and Moira. She had never seen me do any public speaking either, so as I sat in the car with the pair of them, I could be in no doubt that the task ahead of me was an important one. Their presence made me incredibly nervous.

The event was at lunchtime, but we arrived early to meet the other speakers and the chairman of the IOD. When we got there, there was this huge reception committee.

'This can't be for me?' I said, slightly hoping that maybe it was. Then I spotted President de Klerk and realised what the fuss was about. Nevertheless, I set about shaking everybody's hand as if they had turned out for me. A bit cheeky, I suppose, but there you are. I made some small talk with the director of the CBI as we counted down the minutes in the green room and tried to suppress my nerves. My father and Moira both wished me luck and then went to take their places at one of the VIP tables. I was left alone for a few minutes to go over my speech for one last time. 'As long as they laugh at the jokes', I told myself, 'I'll be fine'.

This was the very first Ratners shop which my father opened in 1949 in Richmond, Surrey. It was re-sited 5 years later.

This is me on my very first day at work in the Oxford Circus branch of Ratners - I loved it from day one, despite not looking too happy in this shot!

With my parents in London in the late 50s aged about 9 - I am holding a monkey who seems to have taken a liking to me.

It was an enormous privilege to meet the Queen when I was invited to a reception at Buckingham Palace for business leaders and politicians. The man in the middle is Tony Berry of Blue Arrow.

It was exciting to be part of 'Thatcher's Britain' and in 1989 I was invited to a private lunch at No 10, hosted by the PM herself. I remain a big fan of 'The Iron Lady'.

Photo used with permission of Mirrorpix.

Photo supplied with permission of NI Syndication.

The morning after the day before.... These were the headlines that greeted me the morning after my 1991 IoD speech.

"AH, YES... A GENUINE RATNER... I CAN READ THE HALLMARK... C...R...A...P!"

The Press never missed an opportunity to joke and point fun at my mistake - and some were very funny indeed. (Cartoon by Tom Johnstone, published by *The Sun*.)

I launched GeraldOnline in 2004 after discovering that 'Ratners' was still the most recognised name in jewellery by consumers. For legal reasons, I wasn't allowed to use 'RatnersOnline' but GeraldOnline is now an enormously successful business. It's great to be back in the jewellery business. (Photo supplied with permission of Bucks Free Press.)

It sounds corny to say it, but I really did 'find myself' again through cycling. I now do 28 miles per day, every day of the week come rain or shine.

Here I am presenting Terry Leahy with the Grocer of the Year Award in 2005 when Tesco had become a huge force in UK retailing.

I get asked to do a lot of public speaking these days. The IoD asked me back in 2005 to talk about my experiences since that fatewell day at the same venue in 1991. In the background here you can see one of the publicity shots I did for *The Sun* when I was trying to crisis manage the situation - it didn't work! (Photo supplied with the permission of Tony Cooper.)

I've always enjoyed skiing and our family go every year. This is a shot taken in 2002 of myself and Michael Green, my friend from boyhood who went on to be chairman of Carlton Communications.

Some years we like to spend Christmas in Scotland - here is the whole family attempting to pose for the camera. From the back: Sarah, Alfie the dog (just visible nibbling my ear), myself, Suzy, Lisa, Jonny and Moira. Happy times.

CHAPTER 19

That Speech

I knew the reason I had been invited to speak was because the audience wanted to know why Ratners was continuing to perform so well when our competitors had faltered. We had just posted record annual profits of £130 million and I wanted to show that it was down to two major factors – our presence in America and the fact that in the UK we covered the entire market from luxury watches to the kind of jewellery you wouldn't mind if you lost in a nightclub. I talked about how we had 50% of the UK market and had grown our share of the US market from 4% to 12% in just a couple of years. I told them about our concession in Bloomingdales in New York and our Watches of Switzerland division, which had been part of the H. Samuel deal and sold a pocket watch for £500,000. To demonstrate the breadth of the company, I went on to say that in Ratners, we also sold a pair of gold earrings for 99p. Then I made my joke about the prawn sandwich, and as soon as it got a laugh, I started to relax and enjoy myself. I then told them that we didn't just sell jewellery, but gifts too. I highlighted the sherry decanter. I made a mistake and said that it sold for £4.95 instead of £9.95, but it didn't matter: the 'crap' punch line got another laugh.

I moved on to talk about our staff incentivisation schemes and how we had the best team in the world and how I loved working with such talented people. No one remembers that now of course, but that's what

I really wanted to get across in my speech: sure I had a great business as far as the balance sheet was concerned, but I wanted them to know I had a great business in every other sense too. I wanted them to know just how much I loved Ratners.

At the end of the speech, there was a standing ovation – which I wasn't used to – and people came up to me and said how much they had enjoyed it. By the time I sat down I felt like I'd shaken hands with every person in the Albert Hall! When I took my place at our table, the sense of relief was incredible and I felt fantastic. I had no sense at all that the speech had been anything other than a success. I might even have gone as far as to say it had been a triumph.

Afterwards, there was a small question and answer session in a side room where most of the questions were asked by a group of children who had been there on a school trip. I made a few more jokes and then said that I had to leave. Just after I had said goodbye to everyone, a journalist from the *Daily Mirror* ran after me.

'Aren't you making fun of your customers?' he asked me.

'What are you talking about?'

'You knowingly sell your customers crap. Don't you think that's making fun of them?'

'No', I said, a little confused by the accusation. 'No I'm not, I was just making a joke and having a bit of fun.'

'Mr Ratner...'

'I really have to go now.'

Moira, my father, and I got back into the limo and went home. I was completely exhausted, the nervous energy that had kept me wired in the days beforehand had been spent and I just collapsed on the bed. I'd not been home long when Charles Saatchi called.

'There's a fantastic piece in the *Evening Standard*', he said. The first edition of the *Standard* comes out at 11am, so obviously the journalists had written a piece from the draft of the speech the IOD had issued. 'There's a good line about you calling some of your products crap. It works really well. You come across as a really great guy with a good sense of humour. It's terrific PR.'

This obviously put me in a good mood, but I was still shattered and needed a couple of hours' kip. Later in the afternoon, I got up and started getting ready for dinner. Moira and I had arranged to go out for a meal with the *Sunday Times'* business editor Jeff Randall and his wife. Towards the end of the meal, Jeff came back from the loo and told me there were journalists outside waiting for me. He'd obviously recognised one of them and had spoken to them. His face told me they weren't there to congratulate me. If I'm honest, I was still on too much of a high to think that they could possibly write anything negative – after all, it was a speech I had practically given verbatim several times before. If there had been anything scandalous about it, surely they would have already written about it?

As we left they asked me: 'Do you regret what you said?'

I was a little stunned: 'No, not particularly.'

'Do you mind if we take a picture?'

'Sure, go ahead.'

When we got home about 11.30, I began to worry about what the press were up to. I couldn't sleep, so I drove to Victoria Station where I knew they always got the early editions of the papers first. This in itself was quite an unusual event – I didn't often drive myself in those days, but the chauffeur had long since clocked off. The optimist in me actually thought they might have written something flattering.

All they had at that hour was the *Sun* and *The Times*. I found a bench and flipped through them. There was nothing in *The Times*, and just a little piece in the *Sun* that mentioned the 'crap' line. I told myself it wasn't too bad. I could live with a little bit of bad publicity in the *Sun*, so I drove home and went to bed.

In the morning, I went to the garage across the street where my driver was waiting with my car. He was reading the *Mirror* and holding a copy of the *Sun*. When he saw me, his face fell.

'Good morning', I said.

He didn't say anything and just handed me the papers.

The front page headline in the *Sun* was 'CRAPNERS'. The *Mirror's* front page screamed 'YOU 22 CARAT GOLD MUGS'. Clearly the *Sun* had seen the *Mirror's* first edition and changed their front page.

I was so shocked, and weirdly scared, that I started shaking. The story continued on page three in both papers. The story was basically the same: here was this guy who's company is worth hundreds of millions of pounds who's making fun of his customers and enjoys selling crap. They were effectively telling their readers that they would be idiots to buy anything from me ever again.

I didn't know what to do with myself. I felt I couldn't sit still long enough to be driven to work so I told the driver I would walk to the office. I managed to cool off a bit by the time I arrived, but I couldn't shake the sensation that everyone was looking at me and wondering if the things in the paper were really true. I felt incredibly exposed and rushed straight into my office without talking to anyone.

The phone didn't stop ringing. Occasionally it was friends and family trying to find out what was going on, but mostly it was different journalists looking for a quote or offering a profile that 'would set the record straight'. The constant offer of bargains and threats left me feeling assaulted. All I wanted to do was put bars on the windows, shut the door, and disappear until it blew over.

By the afternoon, the international press had started calling and I realised this was a story that wasn't going to go away. Earlier in the day my secretary had taken a call from the producer of *Wogan* asking me to go on that night's show. By the middle of the afternoon, I had accepted.

Wogan, Terry Wogan's three-times-a-week chat show, was a national institution with millions of viewers in the early Nineties. As it went out live, I knew I couldn't be stitched up in the editing. Once I'd made the decision, my office gradually filled over the next few hours with staff and friends offering advice on everything from what to say to what to wear. Tim Bell, the PR expert, phoned up offering tips. Michael Green called, Victor was on the speaker phone most of the afternoon. I had plenty of advice, but none of it was particularly helpful. By the time I turned up at the Shepherd's Bush studios for the recording, I had been so bombarded with advice that I barely knew which way was up.

I later found out that the producers had bumped a boy band to make room for me. I was the hot story of the day and was Terry's main guest. To his credit, he could see the comments I'd made for what they were, jokes; but he still had to ask me all sorts of questions about our merchandise that – if I answered truthfully – didn't make me look good. I just wanted to say: what do you expect for 99p? If anyone bought those earrings or that sherry decanter, they must have been deluded if they thought they were buying quality. They were buying cheap, largely disposable, gifts that weren't designed to last. But, of course, I couldn't say anything like that. I had to say things like 'competitive', 'impulse purchase', and 'cost effective'. Suddenly I didn't really sound like me, I sounded a bit like one of the fat cats I was accused of being.

What I didn't realise until the following day was that going on *Wogan*, far from helping, only made the situation worse. All I had done was alert millions of customers who hadn't read the papers to what had happened. A disaster was quickly turning into a tragedy.

A couple of days after the speech, many people – myself included – were surprised to see that our share price hadn't collapsed. It took me a couple of days to come up with a theory: we had a trip planned to take a group of analysts to see our operation in America. Usually companies do this when they're about to make an announcement, so brokers were buying our shares, or holding on to them, in case we were about to release a statement that would see our price leap.

I remember meeting one of the analysts at Heathrow for the flight out. He told me his taxi driver hadn't stopped talking about me the whole way there. As everyone knows, London taxi drivers are a pretty good barometer of public opinion: if everyone was as outraged as he was, I knew I was in trouble.

The trip to the States ended without me making an announcement about another takeover or merger, and on our return to Britain, our share price began to drop. That wasn't the worst thing though. The tabloids continued their campaign against me and I began to feel victimised. The *Sun* printed a picture of my house under the headline 'The house that crap built'. If it had been anyone else, I would have laughed too, but it really hurt and I had trouble seeing the funny side of it. On another day, the house in Bray was pictured alongside the house in Mayfair, which was next to the boat, which was next to the helicopter. They were trying their hardest to paint me as a tycoon who had squandered his customers' money on unnecessary luxuries.

The broadsheets got in on the act too. A cartoon featuring Neil Kinnock – whose leadership of the Labour party was being called into question ahead of the 1992 election – showed him on a window ledge preparing to jump. Someone inside the window looked like they had come to talk him down. Instead the caption read: *Would you mind getting off the ledge because Gerald Ratner wants to jump off.*

At the time Ratners sold a gold chain that we advertised as unbreakable. It had been made using laser technology which meant none of the links had joins, which made it much stronger. One of the papers, I can't remember which, tied one end of a chain to one car, and the other end to another car, then drove the cars apart. Of course the chain broke. 'So much for Ratners crap' read the headline.

It's really quite difficult for me to explain just how much these kinds of attacks hurt me. It wasn't just my company that was being lambasted, it was my *family's* company, the company I had grown up in and loved. It was like watching your child being bullied and being unable to help. And of course, as the company's name was the same as the family's, it wasn't just my company that was suffering, it was my children. Virtually overnight, our surname became synonymous with crap. No one can imagine how I felt at letting my father down like that. And my poor daughters were teased and taunted. I took comfort in the fact that my mother hadn't lived to see it.

I really knew I was in trouble when Michael Green let me win at tennis. We played fairly regularly, but the week after the first headlines appeared, I beat him for the first time in months, if not years.

We were both very competitive, and normally if I was ahead, he would raise his game and use tactics that would ruin my chances. It was the kind of sympathy that made me very uncomfortable.

Tennis aside, Michael was someone who offered unconditional support. He reminded me that Moira still loved me, my friends still loved me, and that they were the people who mattered, not the readers of a newspaper I would never meet. He was right, but it was hard to believe him when the taunts wouldn't stop.

It was clear that I had become a liability to the company and so I offered to resign. There was no way I wanted to go, but I was also pretty sure there was no way my resignation would be accepted. Victor, John, Gary, and the other directors told me to go back to work. 'This won't go on for ever', they said, 'in a few months' time we'll have put this behind us and you should stay around to help us turn the corner'.

I was very grateful for their support, but there was no doubt that the press furore was weakening my position within the company. We had just negotiated a new deal with Rolex for our Ernest Jones shops, and the *Sunday Times* wanted to come round and take a photo of me wearing a Rolex.

'No way. Call them back and tell them you won't do it.' Victor was unusually insistent. 'Under no circumstances do I want your picture, your face, connected to Ernest Jones.'

He was right of course, but before the scandal had hit, I would have been much less likely to listen to him. With the continuing media assault, however, the last thing I needed was to cause unnecessary internal ructions. Needless to say, I called the *Sunday Times* and cancelled the photo shoot. It was a shame, because I needed some good press.

After a couple of weeks of negative media comments, I couldn't take any more. I called up Kelvin Mackenzie who was the editor of the *Sun* at the time. Keeping a calm voice was a struggle when I was so full of rage for this man who had put my daughters' happiness in jeopardy.

'Could you stop doing this now', I said. 'It started off as a joke but it's just not funny any more. My children are being called names and, quite frankly, I'm starting to lose my business which means lots of people will lose their jobs.'

'What you failed to realise Gerald, was the power of Ratners, what a huge brand it is and what a big story this is.'

'Well, you've had your headlines, now I'd like to get my company back.'

'Well you should apologise then.'

'OK, I'll apologise.'

'I'll send a journalist over.'

He was a very direct man, he still is if his TV appearances are anything to go by, and there wasn't any chitchat. The journalist and photographer turned up an hour or so later.

When they took the photo to go with the interview in which I apologised for selling cheap jewellery at cheap prices, which had never previously been a crime, they handed me a toy gun and asked me to point it at my head. I obliged, and the next day they ran an 'exclusive' interview with the 'disgraced' fat cat and that photo took up half the page. The image still crops up from time to time. It's like it's haunting me.

Over the next few weeks, I began to understand why comments I had made without incident for the past five years had suddenly become news. Britain was in the middle of its worst recession for a generation and home owners were struggling with massive mortgage payments and negative equity. People were being laid off and salaries were depressed: some people were really beginning to suffer, and so the sight of me with my houses and helicopter was an insult to what a lot of people were going through.

The term 'fat cat' was applied to anyone seeming to be doing well at others' expense. Before me they had laid into Nicholas Goodison, the chairman of the Stock Exchange, but because his name wasn't also a high street name, it wasn't such big news. Journalists were like sharks, preying on anyone in danger of making a mistake, and although it was primarily the chief executives of the privatised utility companies that came in for their venom (Cedric Brown at British Gas was the scalp they really wanted), none of them had made a speech that could have been construed as making fun of their customers. I got the distinct impression that the tabloids had just been waiting for a high-profile businessman to make a mistake. Like a pride of lions, they separated off a vulnerable target and then mercilessly pursued it. I was deemed an acceptable target because I had 'used' the press in the past to float suggestions about takeovers and mergers and to raise my profile. The old adage that they build you up to tear you down certainly seemed to be true.

The apology in the *Sun* kept the tabloids at bay for a while, but the damage had already been done. After those initial couple of days, our share price had continued to fall. I had never been too worried about the share price as I never owned that many shares, but the news from the managers in the Ratners shops was that sales were starting to be hit. The one silver lining was that because so much of the furore had been directed at me, it was only Ratners shops that got the reputation for selling crap. H. Samuel, Ernest Jones, Zales, and our other brands were largely unaffected. I was so glad that we had never got rid of the H. Samuel brand, as there had been a point when we'd briefly considered it: in the past I had done so many interviews – in magazines, television, and radio – and whenever I appeared, Ratners got a boost because of the name. H. Samuel managers had begged me to rebrand. Thank goodness we didn't. The irony was, of course, that the bloody sherry decanter had been an H. Samuel line! But because Mr Hussein had got me to tweak the speech at the last minute, the quote kept reappearing that it was Ratners that sold crap. Of course, that got twisted and misquoted, and it became widely believed that I had said our jewellery was crap when I had never said such a thing. To this day people still think that's what I said. As the saying goes, never let the truth get in the way of a good story.

At first our sales only dipped slightly. We were insulated from the worst because many jewellery purchases are planned weeks in advance, and when people have chosen the ring or gift they want, they tend not to change their mind. However, I heard a couple of stories from my managers that men had gone into Ratners to buy an engagement ring, but then gone straight into H. Samuel and asked if it would be possible to buy one of their presentation boxes. Giving a Ratners ring was no longer considered very romantic. Things were going to get worse before they got better.

Within a few weeks of those first headlines, the sales figures in the Ratners stores entered a terminal decline. At first it was a 10% drop, then it slipped to 25%, then we just about broke even, but within six weeks or so, we were losing money. It didn't help that customers who had bought jewellery before the speech were now bringing their purchases back and asking for refunds. I had always been amazed at how quickly you can implement changes in retail – in the past, decisions made on a Tuesday had paid dividends in Saturday's sales figures – and now I was experiencing the other side of the coin. It's really quite frightening how vulnerable big high street brands are, and I bet few of the people who run those organisations today realise it.

I went to see our managers to find out if there was anything we could do differently. They told me that they were getting so few customers through the door that they weren't even getting a chance to sell anything. All we could have done was put bigger and brasher posters in our windows, but then that would have made us look like the cheap, market stall traders the press had branded us as. Morale was terrible: managers who had previously treated me like an old friend now saw me as a traitor. Many of them believed I had said that our jewellery was crap: 'How do you expect us to sell anything now?' they asked.

I wrote a letter to all our managers to give to our customers. It explained that the press had exaggerated what I'd said and apologised if anyone had thought I had been making fun of them. Copies of it went in the windows, replacing our '50% off' posters, but it didn't do any good.

On a visit to our Nottingham shops, I saw something in the window of Beaverbrooks, one of the larger of the independent jewellers, that made my blood boil: it was the front page of the *Sun* screaming 'Crapners'. I had known the family that ran Beaverbrooks for most of my life, and this gloating at my misfortune was incredibly hurtful. I phoned Michael Brown, who was in charge there, and told him I thought it was a dirty trick. He stopped short of an apology and blamed the local manager: it was pretty clear my rivals would use my misfortune as a commercial opportunity. If one of my rivals had hit the ropes so publicly, would I have tried to capitalise on it? Not if it happened now.

Interestingly, it may have been that their tactics backfired. Rivals who I had taken business from for the past six or seven years might rightly have expected that my customers would now become their customers. However, sales figures for jewellery nationwide were hit and no one picked up our trade: people had been put off buying cheap jewellery altogether. How much of this was the recession starting to bite, and how much was the 'Crapners' effect, I couldn't say.

Although the *Sun* had eased off after my apology, the *Mirror* and *Today* – Eddie Shah's short-lived full-colour tabloid – continued their campaign against me. Journalists were constantly outside my door, chatting to my children and going through our bins. Of course, because the *Mirror* continued its attacks on me, the *Sun* began running stories again so that they could compete with their rivals.

It just so happened that my brother-in-law knew Robert Maxwell, the owner of the *Mirror*, and so I asked him if there was anything he could do. A few days later, I got a call from Kevin Maxwell, Robert's son.

'If this carries on', I told him, 'we're going to have to close shops and make staff redundant and it's going to be your fault'. I told him that a lot of the stuff they had been saying about me wasn't true. Maybe he thought that was a threat that I might get the lawyers involved, but at the end of our conversation he said he would talk to his dad. No one has anything nice to say about Robert Maxwell now, but to his credit, that was the end of the *Mirror*'s witch hunt. It was just the rest of the press I had to worry about. Even *The Times* had taken to calling me Mr Crapner when writing about the company in the business pages.

I felt I had no choice but to call in a libel lawyer. He went through the press cuttings and selected the worst pieces of misrepresentation. He fired off threatening letters, and several papers printed apologies in which they acknowledged that I had never called my jewellery crap. One paper had even made up a quote that had me claiming 'I love selling crap'! Although the apologies were welcome, they appeared at the bottom of page 18 and were about three lines long. Nobody saw them, and a few days later a story slagging me off would be back on the news pages. My lawyer would send another letter, they'd apologise again on page 18, and then they'd stitch me up again whenever they felt like it. All that was happening was that my lawyer was getting richer, so I stopped complaining.

In late July, about three months after the speech, I found myself walking through Hyde Park not far from my house. I remember thinking, how the hell has this ever happened? The months had taken their toll, and I was no longer coping with the strain. First there were the tabloid attacks, then there was the share price, and then there was the downturn in sales. These three things, plus the immense grief I was causing my family, tortured me. I desperately wanted to turn the clock back. I had spent all those years in the Seventies working with my father for little reward, then I'd cracked it and made it a success to an extent I would never have believed. How could I now have thrown it all away? This question rolled over and over inside my mind to the point where I wasn't thinking all that clearly.

The situation worsened when the papers cottoned on to the fact that I owned H. Samuel as well. Sales didn't nosedive, but the weekly figures showed a noticeable tapering off. In some H. Samuel shops, profits were 25% lower in July than they had been in April. Customers were still buying branded watches like Seiko and Accurist, but they were clearly becoming suspicious about our jewellery.

Watches of Switzerland and Ernest Jones, our most upmarket brands, actually did quite well, in part because there was a 'flight to quality', as one journalist put it. I just hoped none of those tabloid journalists were any good at their job: otherwise a tiny bit of research could have damaged those brands too.

If there was one thing my father had taught me about the jewellery business, it was that Christmas was everything. It was now coming up for autumn, and I knew if I didn't have a good Christmas I was finished. The problem I had is that the one thing I had always competed successfully on, price, was now my problem: cheap equalled crap in the eyes of our customers.

My anxieties multiplied when I had a meeting with Gary O'Brien, my finance director. The drop in our share price meant that the value of the company in relation to the vast amount of debt we had taken on to buy Kays was concerning him. He also reminded me that a condition of the loan we had from Barclays was that our profits would not fall below £40 million. To put it in perspective, the previous year we had made £130 million: there was just no way when we had agreed the lending that we thought our profits could drop that much.

'I think you should go and see the chairman of Barclays and explain what's happening', he said.

I went there feeling like a sheepish school boy, but it was actually a constructive meeting and the bank was reasonably sympathetic towards me. 'We're concerned', he said, 'but not tearing our hair out with worry'. The City knew me as an able chief executive, and there were still a few people out there who thought I could turn it around. Luckily, he was one of them.

'I know there's talk that I should bring in a new chairman, a non-executive chairman. What's your view on it?' I asked.

'Well, no one in this bank is jumping up and down and demanding it, but it's probably a good idea.'

I didn't much like the idea of giving up some of the control I had as chairman and chief executive, but I realised the shareholders would like it, and it might help to staunch the flow. I started asking around for suggestions of people I could offer the position to.

My main concern was getting Christmas right, however. We had already started discounting in November to encourage gift buying, but it wasn't doing the trick. Ratners had very little ammunition, and despite my reservations, our only serious weapon was price. People wouldn't mind buying 'crap' if it was cheap enough, so I suggested that we had a massive '25% off everything sale'.

'It'll cripple us', said Mr Hussein.

'It will only be for one day.'

'That could still cripple us.'

'Why don't we just try it out in one part of the country then, and see what happens.'

We decided the one-day sale would be across the whole of Scotland and it was horrendously successful. Customers who had said they would never shop with us again, came in and bought massive amounts of stock. In fact we shifted so much stock that other retailers were affected.

I got a call from Jeff Randall at the *Sunday Times*. 'What's going on in Scotland?' he asked. He sensed a big story: if Ratners could turn around it would be headline news. 'I've had retailers call me and say they didn't take any money on Saturday because their customers had spent all their cash in your shops.'

I thought I had cracked it, and decided to have a one-day sale across H. Samuel and Ernest Jones, as well as Ratners, nationwide. People were queuing up when we opened and when I called a few of the managers to find out how it was going, I could have cried with relief when they told me that they couldn't re-stock fast enough.

Every silver lining has a cloud, however, and this one was about to unleash a downpour. Because the 25% off offer was on top of the existing Christmas discount, we were actually selling some of the items at a loss. What made matters worse though, was that on the weekdays we got even fewer people through our doors: they were all waiting for the next one-day sale.

We tried it again the following Saturday, but our margins were crushed to pieces – just as Mr Hussein had predicted – and if we carried on with it, it would indeed cripple us, just as he had said. I was at my wits end. It felt like I wasn't just losing my grip on the company, or on my personal wealth, but on my sanity. I was a frantic mess, at times enthusiastically talking up the next big impossible plan, and then moments later plunged into the kind of despair that I couldn't see an end to. I don't know how Moira put up with me. Needless to say, we had a bad Christmas, and that meant the new year was not going to bring the company any joy. If it hadn't been for our American division, where my name meant nothing to the customers, we might well have gone under.

CHAPTER 20

As Bad as it Gets

When you're down, it seems you're easy to kick. Maybe it's just that when you're up you can deal with the blows more easily, but I was beginning to feel like I was being kicked all the time. In March 1992, I had a routine check-up at the dentist, and he noticed a strange mark on the roof of my mouth.

'I don't know what it is', he said, 'but I think you should get it checked out. Go and see your GP.'

So I went to my doctor who took one look at it and booked me straight in for an operation to get it removed. I was sent to see a consultant who looked alarmed when I opened my mouth.

'My nephew is a cancer specialist at Hammersmith hospital. I'm going to arrange for you to see him as soon as possible.'

I wasn't sure I had heard him right.

'Sorry. Are you saying I have cancer?' I had only just lost my mother to the disease. I panicked.

'Oh, no, I don't want to alarm you…'

'You failed.'

'… but it seems you have some sort of irregular growth. It might be a melanoma. You should see a specialist.'

'A cancer specialist?'

'Just to be sure, you understand.'

What I understood was that I had just been, clumsily, diagnosed with cancer. I finally understood what people mean by 'the fear of god'. I was terrified. An operation was speedily arranged and I was admitted for surgery. They hadn't done a biopsy, so just in case the growth was cancerous, the surgeon removed quite a large part of the roof of my mouth.

I came round after the operation in the cancer ward. Everyone else in there was terribly ill, and Moira looked very frightened when she came to visit me. When the anaesthetic wore off, there wasn't a pill in the world that would deal with the pain.

I was back at work almost immediately – the company was in such a state that I couldn't possibly stay away from it – and I continued going out to meet the managers and see the staff. When John Hughes and I got in the helicopter to fly to Belfast, the pain in my mouth was so bad I was almost delirious.

We went to see all of our shops in the city, and each manager gave us bad news: sales were down, customers were still angry, morale was low. These agonies compounded the pain in my head. I felt I was going mad and I just wanted to do anything to make the pain stop.

We went to see the manager of an H. Samuel shop, and I was so traumatised I only remember bits and pieces of what he was saying. I understood the basics well enough though: H. Samuel could shift a few trinkets but no one would buy a diamond ring from us any more because they didn't trust the product. A jeweller that can't sell a diamond ring is screwed. As he spoke, I felt something cave in inside me. The pain was so bad I didn't know how I would cope.

'Just give me a minute', I said, and stepped outside into the shopping centre. I remember standing in that shopping mall with my mouth killing me and the overbearing sensation that I had let everyone down. I thought of my father and grandfather building up the business only for me to destroy it. I thought of my kids growing up being called Crapner for the rest of their lives, and I just thought 'it can't get any worse than this'. It was probably the lowest point in my life and I'm just grateful I was on the ground floor. After a few minutes, John came out and we moved on to our next appointment, the despair dissipated with the distraction of small talk and the moment

passed. And a few days later, when the biopsy results came back negative, I belatedly realised just how much of the terror I had felt that day
had been down to the fear of cancer.

A few years later, when I thought about that awful moment in the
shopping centre, I remembered something the pathologist had said
when my sister had died. When they carried out the autopsy, they had
found an infected tooth that had never been treated. She had been in
so much pain, and I realised that must have contributed to her state of
mind when she took the vodka from my father's drinks cabinet.

I had put out a lot of feelers about finding a new chairman, and
although I had talked to plenty of directors from other companies,
none of them had wanted to tarnish their reputations by coming to
such a damaged company. Eventually I took a call from David Alliance,
the chairman of Courtaulds, the big textiles company that supplies
shops like Marks & Spencer. Courtaulds was a FTSE 100 company
and securing someone like David would send just the right message
to our shareholders. His wife was friendly with Moira and I knew him
a little socially. He was a straight-talking Mancunian, although he was
originally from Iran, and I felt he was someone I could trust.

'I've spoken to the City, Gerald, and it's pretty clear to me that they
all still have confidence in you as a chief executive. They have confidence in you as a jeweller and as a retailer.' This was music to my ears.
'I think in the long term, they're not too worried, but a lot of them feel
you need a strong chairman.'

'I agree. I was rather hoping that you were about to offer your
services.'

'I've got someone better for you.'

'Really? Who?'

'It's James McAdam, my Chief Operating Officer.'

'I don't really know him.'

'He's who you need. Trust me. Firm but fair. The City will like it.'

In the days that followed, I asked around about James McAdam,
and I laughed when someone told me his nickname was Mr McKay
after the prison guard in *Porridge*. I invited him to my house in Bray to

see if we could get along, and as soon as I met him, I understood why
he was called McKay: he was a dour Scotsman who wouldn't take any
nonsense. The only problem was, when I was around him I couldn't
stop myself acting the cheeky chappy. A few people started calling
me Fletch. That's when I began to think that we might make a pretty
good double act.

David Alliance had suggested that what I really needed was an executive chairman, but I felt that undermined me too much. However, even
as a non-executive, Jim McAdam would wield a lot more power than
the average chairman: we both knew he was there to make changes.
The first thing we had to do was find an office for him, and the practical solution turned out to be something of a symbolic gesture: we got
the builders in to put up a partition and divide my office in two. My
office at our Stratton Street headquarters was about 60 ft long, so even
when it was cut in half, it was still a decent size. Jim made it clear that
if he was to take the job he would have to be allowed to make some
painful decisions that I and the other directors would have to take on
the chin. I found out exactly what he meant when the first thing he
did was tell me my salary was too high. I had to take a pay cut from
£650,000 to £350,000. I was prepared to do anything to save the company, and so I agreed. He also said that I should not have a five-year
handcuff clause in my contract. 'I'm sorry to have to say this Gerald,
but I guess you're not as valuable to the company as you used to be.' I
couldn't argue with that, and my notice period was cut to three years.
If I'm honest, it was actually a relief to have someone around who was
making decisions: I was unburdened of a little of the responsibility
and it gave me a little bit of space to think more clearly.

Jim spent his first couple of weeks going through our books and
financial records, and after the salary cut, the next thing he recom-
mended was that we sold my house in Balfour Mews. It was a company asset after all. I reluctantly agreed: after all, I had a chauffeur
who could drive me in from Bray every day.

'And that's another thing. You have too many company cars.
Everyone here has too many cars. You can share a chauffeur and I

only want the company to pay for two of your cars. You can either get rid of them, or pay for them yourself.'

Nothing he was suggesting was unreasonable. He was just enforcing the kind of systems that all companies were having to adopt as they faced up to the realities of the recession. It wasn't specific to Ratners, or the jewellery business, it was just common sense in a changed world. It was around this time that I ran into Lynne Franks again. She stopped short of saying 'I told you so', but she did say something that struck a chord: 'All you did wrong was give an Eighties speech in the Nineties.' She was right: the mood had changed and I hadn't noticed it. *Dynasty* and *Dallas* were out, and *East Enders* was in. Margaret Thatcher's ousting from Number 10 had been the end of the Eighties, and the red braces and fat cigars that had become symbolic of the decade. I couldn't help but recognise that I had become joint MD in 1979, just as she had entered Downing Street, and that my troubles began after she had been toppled.

The end of the tax year was looming, and I had more tax to pay than my reduced salary would cover. With the share price on the floor, I couldn't expect a dividends payment to get me out of trouble either. I had two choices: reduce my outgoings or raise my earnings. As the latter wasn't likely, Moira and I discussed our options, and selling the house was the obvious thing to do. We put it on the market and after several weeks, took an offer of £1.5 million for it. This left me £200,000 short on what I'd paid for it.

Over the years I had made some important relationships with bank managers and I found one who would lend me £200,000 more than the value of a new house I had found as my salary more than covered the loan. The new place was only a couple of hundred yards away from the old house, but as it wasn't on the river and was substantially smaller, it cost £375,000. Not many people would move into a house with a mortgage for more than the value of the property, but I didn't have too many choices, and at least I had kept a roof over our heads.

As well as a new chairman, I also employed some new non-executive directors, including Sir Victor Garland, the former Australian High

Commissioner, to win back the confidence of investors. It wasn't like appointing friends to the board who I could rely on to be compliant with my decisions: these directors would vote for whatever was in the shareholders' interests.

Having James McAdam around was a little bit like working with my father again. There was a physical resemblance in that they were both tall and imposing, but his authority fostered a similar sort of atmosphere. Certainly Mr Hussein started seeking approval from him, just as he had my father, and my role became much more about the day-to-day management of the shops again.

The best part of having McAdam on board was that he handled our relationship with the banks. We had loans from a total of 62 different lenders, and if one of them had pulled the plug, then they all would. Our profits had dropped so low that we had broken our covenants with them, and they were entitled to call in their loans. Jim persuaded them all to refinance under a deal managed by Morgan Grenfell. It cost a fortune in fees – around £50 million – and we got hit with higher interest rates, but it kept us afloat.

Nothing Jim could do to the business could alter our relationship with the customers, however. They were still hearing Rory Bremner and Ken Dodd use me as a punch line on TV, and now whenever anyone made a mistake it was called 'doing a Ratner'. This had far more influence on the public than any posters we could put in our windows or merchandise we could source. If things didn't turn around quickly, we would be forced to shut hundreds of Ratners stores.

I remembered how bringing Terry Jordan back in 1984 had made an instant impact. Terry had now retired, and although Victor was still copying many of Terry's techniques, I couldn't shake the notion that a new buyer might be what the company needed. I took the very difficult decision to sack Victor. Not only had he been with the company for a long time, but he was also my cousin. I put it to him that a change of buyer might transform our fortunes, and as his father was still a major shareholder, anything that could boost the share price would ultimately be good for his family. He was given a payoff and replaced by an American who thought he could get hold of different products that would help the public see us a little bit differently.

At around the same time, Mr Hussein announced he was finally retiring. Despite his best efforts with Jim McAdam, it was clear he didn't fit into our more corporate image and he had read the writing on the wall and decided to leave. It was the end of an era, and in many ways I had become an anachronism. The departure of two key allies also meant my only real support at board level was from Nate Lite and Gary O'Brien. Elsewhere in the company, my friendship with John Hughes was also under strain. John had been one of my great friends, and he had been a fantastic general manager, but ever since the IOD speech, he had withdrawn slightly from our friendship and sidelined himself from important decisions. He had been hurt by my speech and I realised I could no longer count on his support. The amount of control I had over the company was waning.

We took the incredibly difficult decision that we would have to close some of our Ratners stores. We had tried rebranding a couple of them as James Walker, an old high street brand we had acquired as part of the H. Samuel takeover, as our PR advisers had suggested a new start. But the fact was – speech or no speech – the recession was kicking in and jewellery sales were fairly stagnant. There hadn't been a year in my whole life that had ended with fewer Ratners shops than there had been at the beginning of the year. Whether my grandfather, father, or myself had been chairman, we had all expanded the company. Now I would oversee a decline. When it's a family company, when it's your name above the door, this actually hurts – but not nearly as much as making people redundant. Letting staff go is one of the hardest things a manager ever has to do. In total we closed 60 branches of Ratners and converted another 60 into H. Samuel or Ernest Jones.

With the axing of our least profitable shops, our figures began to improve and I began to believe that we had turned the corner. I had resigned my other directorships at Norweb, the North West Electricity Board, and from the charity Crime Concern so that Ratners would have 100% of my time, and as long as our American divisions continued to perform well, I still had some personal authority over the company. After all, the expansion in the USA had been my idea, and my success.

At the beginning of 1992 we had predicted profits of $120 million in the USA, but throughout the year that forecast was revised – downwards. By the autumn, my view was that we'd be lucky if we made $10 million, or around $10,000 per store. I still got on very well with Nate Lite, and he reassured me it had nothing to do with my domestic troubles.

'Believe me Gerald, nobody over here has a clue who you are.'

This was oddly reassuring.

The poor performance of Sterling and our other acquisitions was due to just one thing: the recession. In comparison to the UK, the American downturn happened earlier and deeper and every retailer in the States was affected to a greater or lesser degree. We were by no means the worst affected, but because we had borrowed so heavily to make our acquisitions, we were in a lot of trouble. If it carried on, the company would be worth less than the loans we had taken out.

Any chief executive in my position – even one that hadn't made a speech that had brought shame on the entire company – would be feeling vulnerable, but now that our closure programme was starting to see our profit head in the right direction, I felt I was still the right man for the job. According to the City though, my name was still mud, and as my name was the same as the company's name, James McAdam came to me one day and said: 'At the next board meeting, I really think we should talk about changing the name of the company.' I felt sure this was a suggestion by McKinsey, the management consultants McAdam had employed to find a solution to our troubles.

We had our AGM in September 1992, and when there was a higher than average turn out, I knew I was in for a battering. The shareholders tore into me, and of course, the following morning, the press delighted in reporting every word of it. One of the shareholders who got up to speak was a representative of Michael Weinstein who had been given Ratners shares as part of the payment for Ernest Jones. He stood up and said it was 'disgusting' that Ratners had kept me on as chief executive. 'When the *Financial Times* is printing cartoons about your career being in the toilet, you're an embarrassment to every shareholder.' The fact that he was a friend of the Weinsteins made it worse: it meant there were people out there *gloating* at what was happening to me. It's true what they say about being nice to people on the way up, because you're bound to bump into them on the way down.

CHAPTER 21

The End

It seemed, no matter what I did, someone was around to kick me where it hurt and for the 18 months after I made that speech in April 1991, each day spilled into the next with the levels of panic and fear rarely dipping below fever pitch. It is amazing to me that my marriage survived: I was so consumed by work that I had very little left to offer Moira when I got home. She was amazing in those months. Not only was business doing badly, but I was behaving in a bad way. I was so foul-tempered: every time I picked up a newspaper or turned on the TV I would shout at it – someone somewhere would be making a joke at my expense or misreporting what I'd said. At least I could be sure she hadn't married me for the money!

With my mother gone, my father often found himself at a loose end, and he would occasionally come and have lunch with me at my office, just as I had done at his office when I'd run the factory all those years ago. Like me, he wanted to come up with ideas that might help turn our fortunes around, and we would sit with sandwiches at my desk debating the merits of various schemes. He had been in the business too long to dismiss any of his suggestions lightly.

During one of these meetings in October 1992, Jim popped his head through the door between our offices.

'Can I have a word, Gerald?'

'Sure. We're nearly done. I'll be in in a minute.'

When my father left, I went into Jim's office. He looked up at me from his desk with a frown.

'What's up?'

'Take a seat, Gerald.' He had never sounded more like Mr McKay. 'Gerald, I'm going to get rid of you. It just isn't working.'

Unlike Fletch, however, I didn't have a funny line to come back with. I knew he was serious. 'But I've done everything you've asked me to do. I've stayed out of the papers, we've brought in McKinseys, we've re-financed, I've sold my house, we've shut shops. What else could I have done?'

'I'm going to pay you off and I would like you to leave immediately.'

'But we've started to turn the corner. We're through the worst.'

'I realise this must come as a shock to you.'

He wasn't wrong: I hadn't seen this coming and was so taken off guard that I didn't really know what to say.

'What about the rest of the board?'

'There will be a board meeting tomorrow where this will be discussed. Feel free to raise the issues you've just mentioned with everyone else tomorrow.'

The board was now so weighted in his favour that I didn't much like my chances of persuading them that I should keep my job. The following day, I waited in my office like a lemon waiting to be called. I wasn't able to phone anybody or talk to anyone within the company, I couldn't even write to anybody. I just stared into space as they kept me waiting for eight hours. It was late evening when they finally asked me to join them. It took around 15 minutes for them to confirm what I already knew: I was fired.

I was allowed to keep my car, though not the driver of course, as part of the severance package and so I drove myself home to Bray through pouring rain. Just beyond the M25, a light came on on the dashboard: I was nearly out of petrol. I found a station just in time, and as I pulled up to the pump I realised I didn't know what side the petrol cap was on: the chauffeur had always filled up. After a bit of fiddling around, I eventually got the petrol cap off, but it had been years since I'd used a petrol pump and I only succeeded in covering myself in petrol.

I sat in my car and thought about Mr Hussein who had left the company a few months beforehand. He had been given a leaving party, and presents, and a cheque. I hadn't even had the chance to say goodbye to people I had worked with since the day I left school. I began to cry for the first time since Murphy my beloved beagle had died. I think there was just something so unexpected about both events that my body went into some kind of shock, and I was unable to hold back the tears.

So I arrived home, red-eyed and drenched in a highly flammable liquid that had ruined my clothes, to a house that was worth less than I'd paid for it, fired from the only job I'd ever had, with my reputation in tatters. I felt sorry for myself, but I was also incredibly angry.

I had worked bloody hard for 30 years, making millions of pounds for shareholders and creating thousands of jobs for a company I loved, and I had suddenly had it taken away from me. Not for doing anything criminal. I hadn't embezzled. I hadn't lied. All I had done was say a sherry decanter was crap. The pay-off would barely cover my negative equity and the coming year's school fees. I wasn't just unemployed, believe it or not, I was penniless.

Unable to make conversation, I flipped on the TV and caught the *News at Ten*. Towards the end of the bulletin, there was a short piece on my departure from Ratners. The board had had to make an announcement before the markets opened in the morning, but they clearly hadn't wasted any time if they'd made the deadline for the *News at Ten*. The newsreader also announced that the company's name would be changed. Ratner was now a name that brought embarrassment to everyone who used it, and the group would now be known as Signet. Watching your demise on TV is a little like being present at your own funeral – and it isn't something anyone should live to see.

CHAPTER 22
The Wilderness

The following morning, I was woken up by the phone ringing. It was Charles Saatchi.

'Have you seen the papers?'

'Not yet. What are they saying about me now?'

'Actually they are being pretty kind.'

'I guess they've finally got what they wanted. They'll probably lay off me now.'

We spoke for maybe 20 minutes. He agreed I should get a lawyer to review and perhaps fight the terms of my termination, and he was very sympathetic.

'What are you going to now?'

'I was talking to Moira about this last night.'

'Yeah?'

'Yeah, I'm going back into the jewellery business.'

'What?'

'There's a shop going in Reading. It's not far from here. I'm going back to my roots.'

'Wow.'

'Yep, I'm going to do it all over again.'

There was a pause.

'Gerald?'

'Yes.'

'Do yourself a favour. Don't do that. Take a holiday.'

I guess you could say I took a holiday for the next five years.

I flew with Moira and the kids, my father and his new girlfriend (who I had never met before) to Barbados. We checked into the Sandy Lane hotel, which is just about the most expensive hotel in the world. Obviously I couldn't really afford it, but I just needed to go somewhere where I knew everything would be taken care of: I didn't have the capacity to make any other decisions, and as soon as we got on the plane, I knew I could just switch off.

It turned out that the plane was full of journalists on a press trip, so of course they all wrote about me drowning my sorrows on the beach, but as the Sandy Lane is a private resort, they couldn't bother us once we were there. I passed the days in a haze, sometimes playing Scrabble with my father's 80-year-old girlfriend, but mostly just staring out to sea. I wondered if I should have taken the shop in Reading. After all, it was in the run up to Christmas. In six weeks' trading I could have taken a year's worth of money. I'll never be sure if going on holiday was the right thing to do, but when you've been through trauma – whether that's bereavement or divorce or public humiliation – there's something to be said for just taking the time to cool down.

Taking time out wasn't in my nature. If I had an idea, I liked to act on it instantly – I used to go mad when one of my early financial directors said 'let's reflect on it' whenever I made a suggestion – but I had a lot to reflect on at that point, and taking time out was probably very necessary. I could easily have made a bad decision and compounded my situation by doing something hasty. I'm pretty sure Charles' advice to take a holiday was good advice, but there's still a bit of me that's curious to know what would have happened if I'd taken that shop in Reading.

What I didn't realise at the time was that I was actually going through a type of mourning. I realise it sounds very extreme and probably a bit self-indulgent to say it, but I really was grieving for the loss not just of my job, but of something that had been such a huge part of my life since the day I was born. I was also in a state of shock: trying to keep everything together for the previous 18 months since I'd made the speech had been incredibly stressful. I probably needed that time off to let go of the strain.

When we returned to the UK, just before Christmas, I found it very difficult to know where to start beyond asking my lawyer to look at my legal case and assess where I stood regarding my notice period. However, after a couple of very expensive phone calls – his fee was several hundred pounds an hour – I was informed that no one ever got their entitlement. The money I had been paid already was all I was going to get. That meant I would have to try and find a job, but as my name was in tatters, there weren't any offers coming in. My Ratners shares had once been worth £8 m, now their value was barely over £100,000, however I needed the money and I told my broker to sell them. Just about the only thing I was capable of doing was moping round the house. I used to joke that my first wife threw me out because I was never there: my second wife nearly did the same because I was always around.

I received several supportive phone calls from people I had met over the years, people like Irving Gerstein from Zales in America who told me 'We live in interesting times'. People found it difficult to know what to say, but their good wishes and encouragement were genuinely soothing. Knowing that not everyone thought I was a complete waste of space was something I needed to hear, especially when I would occasionally receive letters from shareholders and customers telling me what a terrible person I was. I also couldn't help but notice that we had stopped being invited to quite so many events: it seemed people I had thought of as friends – although not any of my close friends – had disappeared off the face of the earth.

I was so stunned by what had happened to me that it was impossible to see a way forward. Not only had I lost my job, but I had lost the only job I had ever wanted. When I'd been a little boy, I had wanted to run Ratners. I had never had any other ambition. It had consumed my thoughts and my energies for so many years that I had never stopped to think about what I might do afterwards. It was a job I had thought I would have for life. It's difficult to explain, but I felt that I had lost my future, that all the events and milestones I had mapped out for myself had faded. And without the structure and support network – chauffeurs, secretaries, accountants – and a full diary of meetings, my life seemed incredibly empty. Like many men of my generation, I had let myself be defined by my job, and without it I really didn't know who I was.

Moira saved me. She started sending me out on errands – to pick something up from a shop in Henley or Marlow – and so that I would be out of the house for longer, I cycled. This began my latest obsession, and for the next 15 years, cycling would remain an important part of my life.

Something physical happens to you when you exercise, you release endorphins that make you feel better. They've been known to numb pain, and that's exactly what I used cycling for. When I came to a hill, I pushed harder and harder until my muscles hurt, and then, at the top of the hill, the euphoria was intense. Not only did cycling get me out of the house – often for hours at a time – but it blotted out the pain. Other people turn to drink, I turned to exercise.

Moira would also leave me alone with Sarah and Jonny, and spending time with the kids was entertaining, exhausting, and rewarding. On those mornings when Moira went to the gym or met up with friends, I found my time with Sarah and Jonny went very quickly and I didn't have time to think about what had happened to me. I also had much more time to see my older children, and I considered myself very lucky to have four such wonderful kids.

Over time, I began to feel almost relieved that the pressure of meeting brokers' targets, of keeping the gearing at the right level, of repaying hundreds of millions of pounds of loans had been lifted. I started to relax a little, having not ever realised that I had been so stressed – and in a way, it was a little bit like being on holiday. The realisation that I didn't need a job to define who I was dawned on me very slowly, but I did begin to get a sense that the worst was behind me.

A couple of weeks after I lost my job, I had received a phone call telling me that one of our longest-serving managers had died. I wasn't sure if the staff would be pleased if I went to the funeral, but I really wanted to be there to show my respect. It was a bit awkward for some of them, but many of them came up to tell me how sorry they were that I had left. For years, I had been the only member of the board – apart from John Hughes – that they'd had anything to do with. It had always been my job to visit the branches and I had a good relationship with the managers, and now several said they were worried for their jobs but didn't know who to call. Throughout the funeral, I didn't hear the company called Signet once. To them, and to me, it would always be Ratners.

In those first few weeks, I also started doing little jobs around the house. I remember once spending all morning trying to fix the garden hose. It was a task that would have taken most people five or ten minutes, but I had never done any DIY in my life before, and it took me all morning. It was pretty comical, but when I had fixed it, the ridiculous sense of achievement made me realise that life without Ratners might just have its rewards.

It was like I had been in a car crash, or had been a drug addict, and needed rehabilitation. Slowly, through family life and cycling, I began to get a sense that something might lie ahead and that my whole life wasn't behind me. However, I couldn't make a living out of cycling – and certainly not as a handyman – and with my payoff being eaten up alarmingly quickly, I desperately needed a job. My CV, if I'd had one, wouldn't have looked too good. No qualifications, only one previous employer, a reputation to tarnish any company, and no references. I didn't have too many options.

Occasionally a friend or a contact would come and sound me out about this plan or that option, but none of them excited me. We'd sit down with business plans and talk through strategies, but it was usually a case of 'if this went right, and that went right, then you might make £200,000'. It might sound awful, but that just didn't excite me: I had run a company that made hundreds of millions of pounds. A couple of years beforehand, my personal wealth had been estimated at £12.5 million. None of their ideas lit me up like the idea of starting over again and of making another fortune. I had dreams of conquering the world for a second time: losing Ratners had roused my fighting spirit. The same piece of me that had fought to take control of the company, that had fought for H. Samuel, and that had never let go of the Zales deal was now itching to show the world what I could do. I was still only 43, and I became quite confident that I could have a second bite of the cherry.

Yet at the same time, there seemed to be a barrier to doing just that. I felt I was psychologically scarred by it all somehow, and when push came to shove, I just couldn't face going back. I had got out of the habit of working, I had lost momentum, and I was in danger of drifting end-lessly. I used to clip a Walkman to my shorts when I went cycling, and I listened to REM's *Monster* album. There's a track on there called *Let Me In*, and it seemed to sum up how I felt. I was locked out from a world I had been a part of, and just as you always think the party you didn't get an invite to must be the best party in the world, I had this crushing sense of missing out on something. Whenever I would drive anywhere and see one of our stores – I still thought of them that way – I was reminded of what I had lost.

I think the day I most felt like an outsider was the day I opened the paper and read that Signet was closing down all the remaining Ratners shops. They had brought in Diane Thompson – who is now the chief executive of Camelot – as the head of marketing, and she had held a series of focus groups and concluded that the Ratners brand had been so irretrievably damaged that it was no longer commercially viable.

I knew that many of my friends would lose their jobs, but I also felt tremendous sadness that the Ratner name, my father's name, would no longer have a place on Britain's high streets. I just couldn't believe that one speech – two throwaway comments – could have done so much damage. Looking back, I know there's no guarantee I would have kept my job even if I hadn't made the speech. We had been highly geared and suffering a recession on both sides of the Atlantic: our profits would have declined anyway, and our share price would have slumped. But the company could have been restructured, either with or without me in charge, in such a way that the entire Ratners chain would not have had to close. However, the end of Ratners as a valuable brand was absolutely a consequence of my speech and the press coverage that followed it. The rest might well have happened anyway.

CHAPTER 23

Out of the Frying Pan

The news of the closure of Ratners hit me hard. Everything my father and I had built up was being torn down, and I felt a mix of anger and sadness that made me want to get back out there again and prove myself. So when I got a call from an old contact called Sam Nevin who had worked for Ratners' auditors, my ears pricked up. He said a friend of his was interested in offering me a consultancy – I agreed to meet him like a shot.

By now, about three months had gone by since I'd left Ratners and I hadn't had a sniff of an income. So when I learned that Sam's friend, a Scot named Bill Irvine, was being backed by a Kuwaiti oil family, I knew I had to say yes to whatever was being offered. The Kuwaitis had bought land at Tobacco Dock, under the shadow of Tower Bridge. It was a stretch of London that fell between the City and the gleaming new buildings at Canary Wharf. Just about the only landmark nearby was the new offices of News International, home to *The Times* and the *Sun* newspapers that had done me so much harm.

Despite the fact that this was a bit of a black hole for public transport, Bill told me his employers wanted to turn Tobacco Dock into a City centre equivalent of an out-of-town outlet centre. 'We want to make this a destination', he said, 'for office workers to come and buy Chanel and Gucci at prices lower than anywhere else in London'.

We were sitting in the only bar at Tobacco Dock, an awful wine bar called Henry's that was full of *Sun* journalists in suits they hadn't taken to the dry cleaners for years: they were not obvious customers for designer shops. I couldn't fault Bill for his optimism. If I hadn't been so desperate for a salary, I might have thought twice about our chances of success.

Outlet shopping malls were still relatively new in the UK in the early Nineties, and I thought this was an incredibly exciting area to get into. I loved anything that saved the customer money – that had been the driving factor behind my success at Ratners – so I said yes. They were also offering a very generous salary for what would amount to two days a week having meetings with retailers. I could keep my head above water, and still have time for other projects as and when they came along.

My notoriety got them a fair bit of publicity. Some journalists were genuinely interested in what I would do next, and I got some favourable profiles in some of the broadsheets. One of the phone calls I got was from the BBC. They were doing a series called *Trouble at the Top* that followed business leaders as they tried to turn companies around. I was a bit suspicious at first – getting close to the media hadn't helped me in the recent past – but I thought it would be good for Tobacco Dock's profile, so I said yes.

The director, Nick Mirsky, was very careful not to get under my feet when he was filming as I went from meeting to meeting trying to sign up tenants. I arranged for Saatchi's to do our marketing, and they prepared a fabulous brochure that encouraged some of the biggest retailers in the world to set up meetings with us with a view to taking a unit in what would be the most exclusive outlet park in the world. However, a few months into the job, I realised that if I was going to make a success of Tobacco Dock, I would need a miracle. I sensed it was making good television, but possibly for the wrong reasons.

The Kuwaitis were very impressed when I told them a director of Sara Lee – the US cake queen's company had long since diversified into other retail brands – was flying to London with a view to taking six units. If I could get Sara Lee, it would encourage other retailers to follow. Our meeting was at 8am, and so I got up early and drove across London to be at Tobacco Dock to meet him. He still hadn't turned up at 8.30, and by 9am I was quite pissed off. At 10am, I called him.

'So I didn't turn up. Is that really such a big deal?'

I was too stunned to be angry. I just wasn't used to people not returning my calls and missing meetings. I had to adopt a new attitude now that I wasn't the boss, and had to get used to people treating me like I was invisible. It's hard to sell people something they don't want.

I went to France for a meeting with Lacoste, and for some reason Michael came with me. I think we thought we might make a weekend of it, and just for a laugh, he pretended to be my assistant. In the middle of a meeting, Michael started talking about Fred Perry, and the head of Lacoste was lost.

'I have not heard of this Fred Perry.'

So Michael stood up and started miming tennis shots. The Frenchman was bemused to say the least, and unsurprisingly we left without a sale.

I realised there were several reasons why Tobacco Dock was never going to take off. Firstly, exclusive brands like Chanel would rather destroy unsold clothes than let them be sold at a discount. Secondly, any fashion designer who already had a branch in Bond Street or Knightsbridge wasn't going to take a unit: as soon as their customers realised they could save hundreds of pounds for the cost of a £20 cab fare across town, their flagship shops would suffer. The lack of parking was another factor, as was the absence of anything else in the area: there wasn't even anywhere nice to stop for lunch. My days sitting in the empty office there, getting rejection after rejection, were incredibly demoralising.

Sometimes the route I took across London from Bray to Docklands led me down the length of Oxford Street. Old habits die hard: once upon a time, I had loved getting stuck behind the buses so I could see how our shops were looking and to check out the competition. The day eventually came when the three Oxford Street branches of Ratners were closed down. All over the country, they had been turned into branches of H. Samuel and Ernest Jones, or, if Signet could get enough money for the leases, they had changed hands. When I drove past our shop at 219 Oxford Street and saw that it had become a Knicker-box, I became incredibly nostalgic. I remembered playing truant from school and idly walking past it trying not to get noticed, but my sister Diane had been working in there and spotted me. I was taken to see my father, but instead of being told off for playing truant, I was taken out to lunch: he had loved the fact that I loved the shop as much as he did. I hated it that such an important piece of my family history had been painted over. I was so lost in thought at the traffic lights that other cars starting beeping.

The final straw for Tobacco Dock came a year later when I went to a convention for outlet malls in New Orleans. We took a stand and I spent all day talking to prospective clients like a sales rep at the beginning of his career. Some of the Americans had no idea where Europe was, let alone Tobacco Dock, and I came home from that trip with nothing. After two-and-a-half years, I had failed to sell a single unit. The Kuwaitis and I parted company.

When *Trouble at the Top* aired, I was very relieved. Nick had promised that he wouldn't do a stitch-up job, and he had been true to his word. His film actually helped change some of the public perceptions about me: many viewers only knew Ratners as a budget chain of jewellers, and they hadn't realised the company had been so big. Although Tobacco Dock was a flop, the film actually made me look pretty good.

I desperately needed a success. Aside from the money, I needed something that would make me feel good about myself, something that would be a calling card for the rest of my career, something that told the wider world I wasn't a failure. I just had to be grateful that Tobacco Dock had been a fairly low-key failure and not too many people knew about it.

While I was still working for the Kuwaitis, I had been approached by NatWest Ventures, the venture capitalist arm of the high street bank. They had just invested in a French jewellery company called

Cote D'Or and wanted to install their own director to make sure their money was spent wisely.

'No one knows more about the jewellery trade than you, Gerald, and we don't know much so we'd like you to be our man on the ground.'

With Tobacco Dock crumbling around me, the idea of getting back into the jewellery business, where I knew how things worked, was very appealing. It was also wonderful to know that my experience at Ratners – despite the way it ended – had counted for something. However, there were three problems I could anticipate with Cote D'Or: one, I didn't really know very much about the jewellery business in France (and after Ratners' Dutch debacle, I knew enough to be cautious); two, no management team likes a director imposed on them by their investor so I knew there'd be opposition; and three, I didn't speak French. Nevertheless, I said yes.

I went to meet the team in France, and although I got on with them all right as people, as colleagues I knew there was resistance towards me. But there was something about the way the French did business – a long lunch followed by a cigar – that reminded me of how it had been 20 years ago having lunch with my father. After the big City nonsense I'd lived through for the past seven or eight years, a more relaxed way of doing business really appealed. Plus, I loved the romance of Paris – I'd always found it a very exciting city.

They offered me a phenomenal salary – around £300,000 a year – and so I quickly invested in French lessons. A teacher came round twice a week, and in between lessons I worked through a series of CDs. I felt I was making good progress when I chatted easily to my cab driver all the way from the airport to my next meeting. I announced to my colleagues that we could now conduct the meetings in French, but as soon as we got down to business, it was like I'd taken a pill and lost the ability to understand anything anyone said. My colleagues couldn't understand anything I said either. I apologised and we muddled through, mostly because so many of them could speak such good English, but it wasn't fair that they had to speak my language, and it was clear they resented it.

Disheartened, I returned to the UK and tried even harder. My tutor thought I was making good progress, I certainly felt like I was improving, but at the next month's meeting, it was the same story. I began to think they were pretending not to understand me on purpose. At the end of the meeting, I took one of them aside and asked where I was going wrong. Typically, although I had asked in French, I got my reply in English.

'Your French is fine for shopping on the Champs Elysee or ordering a beer and a croque monsieur in a bar, but for business, your French is not good enough.'

'But I can understand everyone I meet, except when I'm in these meetings. I don't understand it.'

'Well, in France we speak two kinds of French.'

'I'm sorry?'

'We have one French for home, and another French for the office.'

No one had ever told me that 'conversational French' was distinct from 'business French': I had been learning the wrong bloody language, and in the process wasting everybody's time! However, I had understood enough of the situation to realise that I had served a purpose, even though I couldn't claim to have achieved very much. I'm pretty sure I was used as a pawn to oust my predecessor and that my main function was as a negotiating tool that allowed NatWest to give him a smaller payoff. I'm not sure they had ever seen me as a long-term replacement, and they weren't too disappointed that it hadn't worked out.

The salary had been nice – it had actually been necessary – but what I had wanted more than anything from my time in France was a success. I had now had three flops in a row, and my chances of ever being employed again were looking extremely slim. I had to do something though, and for the first time in my life, I sat down and wrote job applications. I had never prepared a CV before – I had never needed one – and I had never had to think about what 'transferable skills' I had. It didn't help that the only job I wanted was a job I couldn't have, but a friend put me in touch with a head-hunter with contacts in America. Together we drafted a letter that was sent out to 20 US companies and hedge funds looking to establish a base in London. Within a couple of weeks I had had 20 rejection letters. Although they stopped short of saying it explicitly, the inference was that they'd have to be mad to employ anyone with my track record. Nobody dared employ me, and I had to conclude that I was unemployable.

There was a good side to those few years, however, as I had a chance to do things that I had never done before – going to school plays, taking the kids out, even taking my time over a meal and not having to rush off. I remember being at a friend's house for dinner and actually listening to what the other people round the table had to say. In the Eighties, my mind would always have been somewhere else and I realised I had met many wonderful people that I had never taken the time to get to know. If they hadn't been good for business, I had tended to ignore them.

There were odd little things I noticed too. For instance, I would wait for the lift rather than tearing up the stairs if the doors didn't open immediately. I started listening to music again and discovered bands I hadn't known before. I read sections of the Sunday paper I'd previously chucked in the bin, simply because I had time to. I also noticed that the things I bought changed. In the Ratners hey days, I would have bought the latest camera or Walkman, but they all ended up unused in a bottom drawer. Now I started to buy things I needed, and I appreciated them a lot more.

It changed the nature of my marriage too. Moira and I would talk about things other than the kids and the school run, and we started doing things together. We joined the health club at Cliveden Hotel and made a lot of friends there, many of whom are still friends today. We did things I would previously have pooh-poohed, like wine-tasting holidays in France, and I was a bit surprised to find that I was enjoying it to a certain degree. Just being less stressed opened my eyes to things I had been blinkered to before. Something was missing though, and I just felt I wasn't using my brain. I missed the challenge of business, and nothing I had done with Tobacco Dock or Cote D'Or had come close to the thrill of Ratners. Just about the only thing that came close was cycling.

As I said, I have had a series of obsessions in my life. As a teenager it was Arsenal, in my twenties it was Atkinson Grimshaw paintings, in my thirties it was business. In my forties and fifties it has been cycling, and it is something I have become passionate about.

After a couple of years of cycling seriously, I realised – just as I had learned the wrong kind of French – I had been doing the wrong kind of cycling! I had used a bike I'd bought when we lived in Balfour Mews. In the middle of London there was often gridlock and the only way of getting to a meeting, or going out to the cinema, was by bike. It was a mountain bike that I thought would be suitable for long distances, and I would often cycle to the station in Maidenhead and then catch the train into London. One day the inevitable happened: I got back to Maidenhead station to find that my bike had been stolen.

Now that I cycled every day, I thought it would be worth investing in a really good bike, so I bought another mountain bike for £1500. At that price, I expected a first-class performance, and I decided to try it out by cycling into London on the A4, a distance of about 24 miles. Being on the road with so many lorries was a bit hairy, but it was also exhilarating, and after a 50-mile round trip I felt amazing. I even thought I'd never drive into London again, and for several months I cycled whenever and wherever I could. Eventually the bike needed a service and while I was in my local bike shop, I asked if there was anything I could do to make my bike go faster.

'What are you riding?'

'A Canondale mountain bike.'

'For road riding?'

'Yes. Is that wrong?'

'If you're doing a lot of road miles, you really want a hybrid.'

My new bike, a Dawes, was a revelation. I had no idea cycling could be so comfortable, or so much fun, and it was so fast that it cut 15 minutes off my journey time into London. After that, I just wanted the best bike I could possibly afford, and ended up buying a proper race bike like the kind Lance Armstrong might use. It's carbon fibre, with carbon wheels, and weighs absolutely nothing, which makes it incredibly fast. I can do 60 miles an hour on A roads and it's as smooth as driving a Cadillac.

I've had a couple of accidents, but now that I'm used to the speed, I can get through the smallest gaps in traffic and don't feel any sense of danger. I've upgraded my old Walkman and blast music from my iPod as I ride. The combination of cycling and music is a huge rush, and one of my greatest pleasures these days is discovering new bands. I can't understand men of my age who still listen to the Beatles: I liked them as much as everyone else in the Sixties, but I wouldn't want to listen to them now.

My iPod is very eclectic, and not even my kids have heard of most of my music. I scour the weekend supplements for reviews, and if something sounds good, I'll download it from iTunes, which I think has been one of the greatest inventions of the 21st century. Not only do I rarely listen to music from what people might call 'my generation', but I've noticed that most of the music I respond to is by first-time artists. Maybe it's because they've had to write their stuff without a record company looking over their shoulder, but I have a feeling it's written with more passion. I can hear the hunger and I respond to it. There are very few records that I used to have on vinyl that I've replaced with digital versions. Only Van Morrison's *Astral Weeks* and Joni Mitchell have made it. Friends often express surprise at the music I listen to, but it's really just to do with how curious you are. Many people my age have started to look back; perhaps starting a business again in your fifties, a bit like having a second family, keeps you young?

ACT III

The Rise Again

CHAPTER 24

Starting All Over Again

Health and fitness had become a major force in my life, and I wanted to get fitter and fitter. The facilities at Cliveden were really for the ladies-who-lunch set, and I just wasn't getting a good enough work out. I decided to employ a personal trainer, which I couldn't really afford, to come to the gym with me. She had put a card through my door, and I thought I would see if it made a difference. She made me work out much harder than I did when I was on my own, and I began to see and feel the improvement.

Once I had introduced her to the Cliveden, she advertised on the noticeboard there, and pretty quickly landed herself 30 clients at £30 an hour. She was earning £900 a week, and as soon as I had realised that, I knew there was a market for an upmarket health club with state-of-the-art fitness equipment. Cliveden was too small to have the best range of machines, and its overall ambience was leisure rather than health. The success of my personal trainer convinced me there were a lot of people who took exercise as seriously as I did.

I started telling people who used the club that I wouldn't mind opening my own gym, and one day, one of them told me I should meet a friend of hers. Tony Colbourne lived in Henley, a very affluent town not far from the Cliveden, where there wasn't a gym. He'd had the idea of opening a health club for some time and had actually found a site to build one. I went to see him at his office, which was in a lovely old building that I later found out was mortgaged to the hilt. All over his walls he'd hung picture frames without any pictures in them, which I thought was a bit whacky, but there was something about Tony that appealed to me. He was probably 10 years younger than me, about 35, and was clearly hungry for success. I got the feeling we could make a pretty good team. So he took me to see his site.

It was actually an empty cinema that had been built by John Lewis as part of their planning consents to open a new Waitrose store. As is sometimes the way with facilities the planners have insisted on, they hadn't been able to find a commercial tenant for the cinema and it had been empty for months. It was a terrific place to put a gym as it was right in the town centre and had plenty of parking. As soon as I got back home I picked up the phone, called John Lewis' head office and asked to speak to whoever was in charge of their properties.

Tony and I went to meet John Lewis to discuss the lease, but it turned out to be a very short meeting: they had decided they definitely wanted to find someone who would run it as a cinema, and so we were back to square one. I never gave up on the idea of a health club, so when Tony called a couple of months later and said he had found another site, I jumped in the car and went to take a look.

It wasn't as central as the Waitrose site, but it was still bloody good. It was the first unit on a new industrial estate, which doesn't sound promising for a luxury health club, but because it was the first unit, you weren't really aware of the other units behind it. It was just a mile out of town and also had plenty of parking. It had one huge benefit over the other site, however: elsewhere on the industrial estate was the headquarters of Perpetual Insurance, and this meant hundreds of potential customers who had nothing but a staff canteen to spend their lunch hour in.

'Let's set up a meeting with the estate agent', I said to Tony.

When I got home, I couldn't stop talking. All of a sudden, something that had been an idle notion for a year or more had become very real to me: I could imagine a club at that location, and my mind went into overdrive thinking about the possibilities the site offered.

I imagined a pool, steam rooms, saunas, therapy areas – it was going to be the best health club anyone had ever seen. I must have bored Moira stupid.

In the morning, I called up an architect and arranged a meeting. For a modest fee, he agreed to draw up some initial sketches that would help us convey our plans to banks and potential members. In the meantime, Tony did a rough calculation of what we'd need to convert the warehouse into a gym, and he estimated we'd need around £500,000 (this would turn out to be significantly less than we needed, but it seemed like a reasonable amount at the time). By then, this was 1995, the housing market had recovered, and I estimated I could remortgage and release around £200,000 from the increased value of my house. If Tony could do the same with his place, then we weren't far off what we needed. I was confident I could find people to put up the rest. All we needed now was to secure the lease.

Our meeting with the estate agent didn't go as we had hoped. As a new business with no track record, the owners of the site wouldn't lease the unit to us as we were considered risky tenants.

'However', the agent said, 'they would sell it to you'.

'Well that's something we hadn't thought about, but it might be a good idea. How much do they want for it?'

'£750,000.'

Instead of being put of, or daunted, or dissuaded, I slipped straight back into Ratners mode. The agent had given me a challenge, and there was no way I wasn't going to find the money. I was desperate for another business, and it felt great to be getting back in the saddle.

I started setting up meetings with anyone I thought would help me raise the cash, and at one of those meetings, I got a bit of a shock. I was talking to an old contact, telling him that we needed to raise around £1.25 million.

'I can find the first £200,000', I said, 'and Tony can come up with a similar amount'.

'Are you sure?'

'The figures might be a bit out, but they shouldn't be far off.'

'No, I meant are you sure about Tony?'

'I don't think I understand.'

It turned out that not only was Tony mortgaged to the hilt, but he had also defaulted on his last couple of mortgage payments. I was shocked – he'd never mentioned anything about money troubles. The penny dropped: when he'd heard my name for the first time, he'd assumed that I had a family fortune squirreled away somewhere and that I would be able to bank roll the whole thing. He was almost as shocked by my financial position as I was by his!

But Tony, being an optimist, didn't see a problem: he knew some-one he thought could put up the money. If we could raise £500,000, I was confident we could find a bank that would put up the rest. Tony's contact was a senior executive in one of the big drugs companies that fill the industrial estates in the Thames Valley. He had received a bonus and was keen to invest it, but as soon as he saw Tony's accounts he declared we were a pair of amateurs and pulled out.

No matter how much I liked Tony, it was clear he couldn't help me with my plans to open a health club. I didn't really know the best way forward, but I hoped I would be able to offer him a position as a general manager when I got it off the ground. I felt a bit bad about this – after all, he had found the site – but I couldn't continue with him as a partner.

Being called an amateur really rankled. I had run the world's largest jeweller and had over 2000 shops: I knew what I was doing, and I was determined to prove it. I called Gary O'Brien, who had left Ratners about a year after me. I knew I needed a great team and a great set of accounts if I was to bring in the kind of backing I needed. He'd spent the intervening years as a finance director working for a boss he really didn't get on with. So when I called up and said I couldn't really offer him very much in the way of money, but that it would be fun, he agreed to come on board.

Gary drew up a proper set of accounts that contained my projec-tions on how quickly I thought we could get members. I actually had a pretty accurate idea, as I had started advertising the new club on the assumption that we would raise the money. For the past couple of weeks, the *Henley Standard* had been carrying beautiful ads for the club using our architect's drawings. The advert told readers that if they wanted to see more, they could drop into Tony's office to take a look at the plans. It also told them about our early bird offer: if they signed up now, they wouldn't have to pay the £250 joining fee. I knew we would make a success of the club when I got a phone call from a very excited Tony:

'You're not going to believe this Gerald, but 60 people have signed up today. This one girl came in from Perpetual Insurance. She went back to the office to tell her friends, and the phone hasn't stopped ringing since!'

Even though the club wouldn't be open for another year, there was such demand for a top-quality health club that 600 people had signed direct debit forms. This was the kind of take up that made financiers take notice, and one of the venture capital broker firms Gary had sent our proposal to said he had a client who wanted to meet us. Our potential investor was about to emigrate to Australia and liked the idea of making some of his capital work hard while he was out of the country. He was impressed by the sheaf of direct debit mandates we showed him, he liked the designs, and he liked the size of the profit we thought we could produce. He agreed to put up £300,000.

'I'll call my lawyer in the morning and get him to draw up the papers', he said as we all shook hands.

As I left that meeting, I really got the feeling that opening a club was no longer a dream. With Gary and our new backer on board, it seemed like it was just a matter of time. A few days later, however, I got kicked in the teeth.

It wasn't just that our backer pulled out, it was the reason why he withdrew. Apparently, the lawyer he had called to prepare the investment papers worked for the same firm James McAdam had used when he got rid of me from Ratners. They had seemingly advised our investor 'not to work with Gerald Ratner'. I was livid: if the investor's explanation was correct then James McAdam had now effectively taken two businesses away from me. And it wasn't that I had ever been in breach of company legislation or been anything other than above board. There was no reason for anyone not to work with me, and this made me feel like a financial leper. It didn't help that occasionally someone would come into Tony's office and say something along the lines of 'Weren't you the man who called his customers crap?' and cancel their membership. I felt that I would never get away from my mistake. But worse was yet to come.

The estate agents handling our purchase, Healey and Baker, called: they had other people interested in the unit and they couldn't hang around any longer. They gave me two weeks to raise the money. There was no way I was going to let the health club be my fourth failure in a row, so I went into overdrive.

I called everyone I knew, including an old childhood friend called Lee Marks. Lee's dad Arthur had been my father's best friend, and our mothers had taken us for walks in our prams around Richmond Hill when we were tiny. Apart from family, no one had known me longer.

'It's funny you should call', he said, 'because I was just talking about you the other day'.

'Who to?'

'Do you remember the lawyer Michael Sears, of Sears and Tooth?'

Of course I did, they were one of the biggest firms of divorce lawyers in the country.

'Well, he knows I know you, and he was asking what you were up to. I told him you were opening a gym, and he sounded pretty interested.'

'Could you set up a meeting?'

'I'll call him right away.'

A couple of days later, Gary, Tony, and I went to see Michael Sears in his impressive offices on South Audley Street. We tried not to sound too desperate, and launched into our presentation. We obviously did a good job, because at the end of it, he offered to invest £300,000. As we left, Gary turned to me and said:

'He's even more impulsive than you!'

Our next task was bringing a bank on board for the remainder of the money. I had remortgaged my home and raised slightly less than I'd hoped – £175,000 – which was sitting in the bank, Gary had put in £100,000 of his own money for a 20% stake, and with Michael's £300,000, we needed a loan of about £750,000. With such a huge cash deposit, I really didn't expect too many difficulties as our money would insulate the bank from any potential loss.

Although we were through the worst of the recession by 1996, bank managers were still being cautious. The first one I saw was concerned that we wouldn't be able to meet the repayments until we'd been open for many months.

'But people have signed the direct debit mandates: there'll be an income as soon as we open our doors.'

Although many of the managers I saw were impressed by the number of members we'd already signed up, we were asking for such a large amount of money that they couldn't swallow the risk. By the fifth manager, I was really starting to doubt if we'd be able to get a loan. Gary started scouting round for institutional investors, knowing that time was running out. Then the sixth bank turned us down – we had tried high street branches and international corporate banks, but no one would lend to us. If the big boys wouldn't touch us, I didn't hold out much hope for a meeting with our local branch of NatWest, but I was pleasantly surprised to see that the manager was smiling throughout my presentation. At the end of it, he said yes. I only later found out this was because his wife was one of the people who had filled in our direct debit form. If he had turned us down, I got the impression he wouldn't have been very popular at home.!

When he said yes, I actually felt myself go a little bit weak. I had been so focused on raising the money that I hadn't actually stopped to think about what it would mean to start another business. By this stage, I hadn't worked for 18 months and was running seriously low on cash. Getting the loan was such a relief, but it was also incredibly exciting – I was about to prove that I could start a business from scratch, and not just build up a company I had taken over.

Word got out that I was starting another company, and I got a phone call from the BBC. The same show that had filmed me at Tobacco Dock – *Trouble at the Top* – wanted to do a follow-up. They had been largely sympathetic with the first film, and I welcomed them back with open arms. I wanted more members for my club, and they could provide prime time publicity for free.

I knew it was a risk though. If the health club was a flop that was witnessed by millions of views, I didn't think my reputation would ever recover. I would have to change my name and leave the country if I ever wanted to earn money again.

Much of what went on as we prepared for launch made great television and, unfortunately, what was good for the viewers wasn't always good for my sanity. Michele Kurland, the director, filmed a lot of footage of me rowing with builders and tearing my hair out. Tony's estimate of £500,000 for the building costs proved very optimistic and we needed to save money wherever we could. In our promotional literature, we had promised potential members an out-door pool, and without it it was entirely possible that many of them would cancel their memberships before they had begun. I had to choose between staying within budget or building the pool. I choose the pool.

Some people questioned why I was so dead set on having an out-door pool, but I knew from my research that it would be the key to a successful club. In the 18 months from meeting Tony to getting the loan agreed, I must have visited half the health clubs in Britain. I told them I was interested in joining and was given a tour, which meant I had the opportunity to ask as many questions as I liked.

I was visiting one club in the dead of winter, and at reception I'd been told there was a pool. I hadn't smelt any chlorine as I'd been taken round, and the place didn't have that moist feeling that clubs with pools have. At the end of the tour, the instructor showing me round said 'Would you like to see our pool?'

'I'd love to.'

He opened the door, and an icy blast hit me in the face.

'Are you mad?' I asked, 'Who's going to use an outdoor pool in winter?'

He just smiled and led me outside. I was amazed to see 10 or more people busily doing lengths as steam rose off the surface of the water. It was really quite a beautiful sight and it was clear the members really loved the pool.

'It's even more popular in summer', my guide said.

The reason I was so surprised is that the house we'd moved into in Bray had a pool in the garden, but we hardly ever used it. I realised it was because it was at the end of the garden. The reason the pool at this club was so successful was that it was just a couple of yards from the door. Members rushed out into the cold and couldn't wait to dive into the heated water. There was something slightly anarchic about swimming outside in the dead of winter – it's not even something we do often in summer in Britain – and I realised what a selling point an outside pool would be. I was suddenly taken back to my summers at the Hendon Hall Hotel and remembered just how much *fun* the pool there had been. When I told our architect I wanted an outdoor pool, he thought I was mad. He wasn't the only one, but I placated the team by telling them that if I was wrong, we could always put a roof over it at a later date.

The crew of *Trouble at the Top* liked our pool saga as it was turning into a bit of a farce. They knew we needed one, they also knew we couldn't afford one; so whenever anyone came to give us a quote to build the pool, the cameras were always there. Quote after quote came in at around £120,000, which was near enough a quarter of our budget and we just couldn't afford it. Then, out of the blue, one guy came to take a look at it and said he could do it for £30,000. I was so gobsmacked that I wanted to ask him how he could do it so cheaply, but Tony sensibly stopped me from asking. The only catch was that his quote didn't include the pool house where the filters and thermostats would be kept. As Tony was confident we could find another builder to do the pool house, we said yes to his ridiculously cheap quote.

I also knew a pool would be essential for getting family memberships. There were plenty of gyms that catered well enough for fitness addicts who pumped iron and ran for miles on the treadmill, but there were precious few places where men and women felt equally comfortable working out, and even fewer where they could take their kids. I felt I understood my market very well – I just wanted to build somewhere that Moira and I would take our kids to. That meant having somewhere to eat, somewhere to talk to friends, and a crèche.

The £30,000 quote was the piece of luck we badly needed: there was now no way we would open in the spring as we had planned, but at least when we opened we would have a pool. Content in the knowledge that the launch would go more or less to plan, Moira and I decided we should take a holiday before we opened: if we waited, we might not get a chance for another year.

I left Tony in charge, after all, he was the general manager, and told him the most important thing he needed to do while I was away was to get the pool house built. He promised me it wouldn't be a problem, but of course, when I came back there was no sign of one. He had managed to build a crèche on the cheap, however, by buying the biggest shed I'd ever seen. After a meeting with Gary and Michael Sears, we agreed that Tony really wasn't up to the job. He hadn't invested any money, he couldn't even arrange for a pool house to be built, and yet he was the only one of us taking a salary. It was my job to ask him to leave.

Perhaps it was because we had cameras following us all the time, but Tony decided that what Gerald Ratner's classy new gym didn't need was the bad publicity of a tribunal and he sued us for unfair dismissal. What would be fun for the viewers, was just a major distraction for me when there was so much else to deal with – and so much else to spend our limited budget on – but I felt strongly that we were in the right to let him go, and so we ended up in court. Fortunately the judge saw sense, and declared that we had acted lawfully.

Tony's wife came up to me afterwards and accused me of 'stealing' Tony's business. In a way I was sympathetic, after all, he had wanted to open a gym, and he had even found the site, but he hadn't put any money in, and you could argue, hadn't put much effort in either. He had really thought that getting me involved – me and my imaginary millions, that is – was enough.

CHAPTER 25

The Launch

Even though we had signed up hundreds of customers, to meet our mortgage payments – and make a profit – we needed to sign up two or three thousand. We started advertising the club everywhere we could think of and leafleted just about every house in Henley. On all our publicity material, we announced that we were opening in July 1997. By the end of June, the pool was just about finished, but we still didn't have a pool house, which meant we couldn't fill it. We deliberated – in front of the cameras – if we should open as advertised, even if the pool was unusable. In the end the decision was a financial one: we needed the money, and so the Work Shop opened as advertised in July.

The summer of 1997 was a hot one, and we pretty quickly realised there was something we had forgotten to include in our specifications: air conditioning. I realise people go to a gym to work up a sweat, but there aren't many people who can do an hour's work out in what felt like a sauna. It didn't look good on camera, but at least members would see me do everything in my power to get it fixed. Many thousands of pounds, and a few weeks, later, we had both air conditioning and a working pool, and at this point I started to get letters from members saying how happy they were we had opened.

I really felt we had built the best health club in the country. It was a beautiful building, with excellent facilities and the pool, which opened out on to a patch of woodland, was such a fantastic place to spend time, whether that was sunbathing or burning calories. We had had our teething problems, but after six years in the wilderness, I finally had a hit on my hands. I'd known I could do it, but it was wonderful to be able to show other people.

Although at times the BBC tried to make it look like we didn't know what we were doing, when *Trouble at the Top* aired, we had hundreds of new members come along and sign up. I had been too badly burned to ever believe 'that all publicity is good publicity', but on this occasion, being made to look a little hot-headed on camera had definitely been worth it.

As well as a work out, members also came for beauty treatments. Rather sneakily, I had been using my membership of the Cliveden club to get half price treatments at the beauty spa there. I hadn't really needed a manicure, but I got talking to their beauty therapists and managed to persuade several of them that they'd have a much better time if they came to work for me. We had the best beauty treatments in the area after that, and members started coming in to socialise, not just to exercise.

Our restaurant gained quite a good reputation too, and because we had plenty of parking, members often brought their clients to us for lunch. I loved hanging around in the club, talking to members, meeting friends, and getting to know the staff. Just as I had with the managers and staff in the Ratners shops, I made it my business to know who did what well and who needed more encouragement. By dealing quickly with problems the staff were happy, and if they were having a good time, the members also enjoyed themselves.

Within a few months of opening, we had 2500 members paying £45 a month, which was more than enough to cover our costs and make the repayments on the loan. I started taking a modest salary of £3500 a month, but it didn't cover my expenses which included massive re-payments on the £60,000 of credit card debit I had racked up staying afloat during the construction phase. Nevertheless, it eased the pressure and was a big step in the right direction.

I invited my father to come and see the Work Shop. I wanted him to know that I'd got back on my feet, and I guess I still wanted to make him proud. He'd never been to a health club in his life before, and had difficulty getting his head round seeing people running on a treadmill.

'What are they trying to achieve?' he asked in that blunt way of his.

I had difficulty giving him an answer, and seeing the gym through his eyes reminded me just how much the world had changed in my lifetime. My lifestyle, and the lifestyle of my friends, seemed absurd to him. 'I've heard of people running round in circles', he said, 'but never on the spot'. He thought the exercise bikes were even stranger, but he loved the health club regardless because he could see it was making money.

Just as he was proud of me, I had plenty of reasons to be proud of my own children at the time. Suzy, my eldest, had gone into acting and had landed a part in Guy Ritchie's *Lock, Stock and Two Smoking Barrels*, and in 1998 when it came out, we all went as a family to see it. I hadn't realised she had such a big role, and I got a bit of a shock when she started killing everyone! These days, she mostly works behind the camera, producing and directing TV shows. All of my children have been drawn to the arts, which is curious seeing as they have two different mothers. I suppose they must get it from me and have inherited the showing off gene from my mother.

Lisa has written screenplays and one, called *Suzie Gold*, was co-written with Michael Green's daughter and was made into a film starring Summer Phoenix (Joaquin Phoenix's younger sister). She mostly writes books now. Her younger sister Sarah is still at school and is getting amazing grades, and looks likely to do Theatre Studies at university. Jonny, my youngest, seems destined for a career in the arts too, and I wouldn't be surprised if he ended up on the stage.

One of the greatest things about the health club is that it gave me the flexibility to be around more for my kids. I'm sure I have a much closer relationship with them because I've been able to work around their needs for the past 10 years. And being happy at home filtered through into work: I got a real kick from just hanging out at the club – I think I always arrived in a good mood because it was a 12-mile bike ride from my house – and I got to know many of our members as friends. We decided to have a party to celebrate our first Christmas, and sold all the tickets on the first day: people wanted to spend as much time as they could with us and I took this as a sign that we'd got things right. Whenever I went there, we always seemed to be busy. In fact we were so busy that when Gary gave me the accounts to look at each month, I was always slightly surprised that we weren't making more money.

I started to look at our membership list and saw that a huge proportion of our users had a corporate discount on their rate. Most of the corporate reductions went to Perpetual employees, and at one point I thought we must have had more Perpetual members than they had staff. Something wasn't quite adding up. I spoke to our reception staff and to a couple of members who worked at Perpetual. They pretty much told me what I suspected: word had got out that if you said you worked at Perpetual, you would get a discount. In some cases people had worked there on a short-term contract, but in some cases they had never worked there at all.

That wasn't the worst of it: Gary was waiting for me in my office and looking very serious.

'We have a little bit of a problem', he said.

'Should I be worried?'

'Oh yes. I was out with friends last night who introduced me to some people who use the club.'

'Members?'

'No, that's just it. They didn't know I worked here, and they were telling me about this fabulous club in Henley that they use every night. They were saying how they just walk in without paying and no one ever stops them. What are we going to do about it?'

I really didn't know. When I'd visited all those clubs while I was doing my research, I had never liked the places where you have to sign in, or use a swipe card, and I really didn't like turnstiles. I wasn't running an institute, I was running a club, and I didn't want members to feel like they were being monitored. Besides, our reception was in this beautiful atrium and turnstiles would have looked a mess. We decided to take a relaxed approach to it, and employed extra reception staff whose primary job it was to greet people and ask to see their membership card. Once they had got to know a member, they didn't need to trouble them again. It wasn't foolproof, but it deterred most of the non-payers while still making the Work Shop feel like an exclusive club. It was a compromise I was happy with.

It felt wonderful to be getting back on my feet. In the Eighties I would have wanted to prove something, but in the Nineties I was just happy to be repaying Moira's faith in me and to provide my family with some security. Of course it was also wonderful to own a club – the sociable side of it suited me down to the ground – but my ideas for the club weren't driven by my ego. I had no ambition to run the world's largest chain of health clubs, or for my company to outperform Carlton on the stock market. I had changed since I'd left Ratners, and a modest business was more than satisfying. It probably helped that I was a major shareholder – a position I had never enjoyed in the jewellery business – so even though the club was worth a fraction of the valuation of Ratners, I knew my share in it would be valuable one day. My salary still wasn't enough to cover my expenses each month, but if we could just expand a little bit, I felt I could start paying myself a proper wage and really begin to enjoy life again.

I turned 50 in 1999, and to celebrate we had a party at our house. I didn't have a lot of money at the time, so it wasn't a big event – we just put a marquee up in the garden and asked the chefs from the club to do the food. The important thing was that friends came, and the house was full of people I cared about. There was such a lovely atmosphere that even my children tell me it was one of the best days of their lives. There were a few speeches, but the one I remember was Jonny's. He was only nine, but he stood up confidently and talked without notes. It was a fabulous speech, which made me very proud, and very thankful.

My 50th really felt like something to celebrate. After several years of bad luck and setbacks, I was exactly where I wanted to be, running a business that I enjoyed and surrounded by family and friends. It was a bit of contrast from my 40th birthday when I'd hired a room at Annabel's, the club in Mayfair, and made a speech that succeeded in alienating half of my guests. I'd thought my jokes were funny – there was a stupid gag about a friend who was so mean he'd had his house double-glazed so his kids couldn't hear the ice cream van – but they missed the mark and a couple of people walked out. I should have realised then that speeches can get you into trouble! Looking further back, I can't really remember much about my 30th. Michael Green and I had a joint party at San Lorenzo, but I got so drunk that I may as well not have been there for all I remember of it. Looking back, I see those birthday parties as little illustrations of the different stages in my life: at 30 I was pretty reckless, and 40 I was pretty cocky, but by the time 50 had come round, I was pretty much sorted.

The Work Shop was such a success that we started to look round for another site. I had been approached by Close Brothers, the venture capitalist firm, who said they would be interested in financing our expansion. If we could establish a chain of upmarket clubs in the best areas in the country, they felt we would be onto a winner. I found a site in Beaconsfield, another well-off town slap bang in the middle of the stockbroker belt that didn't have a health club. When I took our investors to have a look at the site, they couldn't see it working and their offer of investment was put on ice. Of course, that site now has a club on it with 7500 members, but that's by the by.

Nevertheless, the Close Brothers' attention had flushed a few other interested parties out of the woodwork. Michael Sears, who had put in £300,000, was keen to see some of the (considerable) return on his investment, and he introduced a couple of people to the club who said they were interested in buying a controlling stake in the business. However, these deals either fell down during the due diligence process or they were never really that serious. Then one day Michael told me he'd like me to meet a contact of his called John West. He already ran a health club and was interested in incorporating the Work Shop into his existing business. Crucially, as far as I was concerned, John was a cash buyer and he was offering £3.9 million for the business. That was the kind of cash I hadn't seen for a decade and my share of it represented a fantastic return on the £175,000 I had put in. I could clear my debts, take a bit of time off, and have enough left over to do something else. I wasn't quite sure what, but I knew John West's offer was too good to turn down.

It got even better when I called my accountant: in the past 10 years I had incurred so many losses that I could offset my Capital Gains Tax. 'Put it this way Gerald, you won't have to pay tax on any of it.'

This was towards the end of summer 2000 and, if the due diligence wasn't unduly held up, then I would get my hands on the cash by Christmas. However, the banks John was using stumbled and stalled on him, and the deal that should have been concluded within a few months dragged on into the new year. At times I wondered if it would ever happen, and just in case it didn't, I began working out how I could buy the site in Beaconsfield and expand the business.

The due diligence dragged on into February, and I was really starting to doubt if it would go through, despite verbal assurances to the contrary. Moira and I had booked a skiing holiday assuming that we could afford it. If we cancelled we wouldn't have got a refund *and* we wouldn't have had a holiday, so we went anyway.

We have always enjoyed skiing together, and we usually go once or twice a year. I find when I'm on the slopes that time goes so quickly, and I was still skiing at 10 o'clock at night when my mobile started ringing. It was Michael Sears in the UK.

'Congratulations Gerald.'

'What's happened?'

'The deal has finally gone through.'

'Really?'

'They'll transfer the money to your account tomorrow.'

I'm not quite sure if I screamed, but it felt like the joy inside me just wanted to burst out. This wasn't just a deal that gave me financial security, it was a deal that put the speech and its aftermath behind me. I hadn't known how much it would mean to me until that call from Michael, and the elation took me by surprise.

That night all I wanted to do was spend money. I went to the supermarket to try and find the most expensive wine they had. I'd have been prepared to pay thousands for a bottle, but the best I could find cost around £60, which didn't seem nearly enough. The next day, the first phone call I made was to Barclays Bank to see if the money had been deposited in my account.

'No Mr Ratner, there have been no transactions on your account today.'

I called back a couple of hours later. 'I'm sorry Mr Ratner, but there's nothing. Would you like me to call you if any money arrives?'

'Yes please.'

I kept checking my phone all afternoon, just in case, as I took Moira shopping. Even though she already had all the ski gear she needed, I wanted to buy her new boots and a new coat.

'But I already have those things.'

'But you can buy anything you want now. We can afford it.'

'I'd rather get back on the slopes.'

I was on a chairlift when my phone finally rang. I was completely enveloped by low cloud and everything around me was white. Something odd happens to sound when you're up a mountain, and it was completely silent apart from the young man from Barclays sounding a bit confused.

'A huge amount of money has been transferred. Is that what you were expecting?'

'It's what I've been waiting for for a very long time.'

It sounds a bit cheesy to say it, but I had made that kind of money before and had never appreciated it. When you've lost a huge amount of money and gone back to square one and made a lot of money again, you really do understand its value. Later that year, when the terrorist attacks on September 11 put the brakes on similar deals all over the world, I was even more grateful. Knowing that I was still capable of making a success of myself was worth about half of the money I'd just received, and of course, knowing that I could buy anything I wanted was an enormous thrill. It's not that I needed much, it's just that I *could*, and after so many years of debt and caution, I happily spent money in restaurants and wine bars all holiday. It was one of the best holidays we ever had because I was just so happy, I completely relaxed and felt an enormous sense of satisfaction.

Later in the year, we took another holiday and went to Portugal, and just as I had been on holiday when Juliet had died, I was away from home when I received a phone call from my sister Denise telling me that my father had passed away.

We had always been closer than most fathers and sons, and as this news was completely unexpected, it hit me like a punch to the face. I flew home straight away determined to find out how the healthy man I had had lunch with just a few weeks before could have suddenly died. I was told that he'd been admitted to hospital a few days previously with what turned out to be a minor stomach complaint. While there, he had caught the hospital 'superbug' MRSA, and had succumbed within a few days. It was such a pointless way for such a great man to die, and it's no wonder that when Tony Blair and Gordon Brown stand up and say what a good job they've done for hospitals that they are greeted with booing across the country. How can it be that you go into hospital to get better and are exposed to something that can kill you: it's an absolute scandal, but it's not just rage I feel, it is grief. My father was a wonderful man who lived quite an extraordinary life, and five years on from his passing, he is still very, very missed.

My faith has played a different role in my life as I've grown older, and as my sister Denise and I prepared for our father's funeral, I was hugely comforted by the structure the rabbi and the synagogue gave us. We didn't have to make too many decisions, because they had been made for us by tradition, and there was a whole community that responds as one at these momentous times in family life. I didn't have my parents any more, but I had their faith and their traditions, and I was quite surprised to realise just how much that meant to me.

In recent years, I have started to become involved with a local synagogue in Maidenhead after having several conversations with the
rabbi there. I had first spoken to him when Jonny was approaching
his teens. I'd toyed with the idea of him converting to Judaism, as
I'd started to feel a sense that he would miss out on something if he
wasn't bar mitzvahed. But for Jonny to convert, Moira would have had
to convert too, and I think that began to seem like too much of an up-
heaval and statement about what were really quite private emotions.

The fact that my wife and two youngest children do not share my
religion makes my relationship with Judaism even more personal.
These days I go to the synagogue occasionally, and help out with
organising kids' parties and things like that. I even did the Kiddush
for them, which involved taking a lot of food for the children, and
leading the prayers. Moira helped me with that – it's a *very* reformed
synagogue! – and she occasionally comes with me to other services.
If Moira can't come, then I tend to go with a friend I know from
North London in the Sixties who has also moved to Berkshire. I
bumped into him after nearly 40 years, and talking to him was easy
and relaxed. I recognised that it was because we shared so much by
both being Jewish, and I think I became nostalgic for something I
had ignored for so long. I have realised being Jewish is part of what
makes me who I am.

CHAPTER 26

Dotcom Millionaire

A number of friends suggested that I put my money from the Work Shop into stocks and shares, but just a couple of weeks after we got back from holiday, the impact of the dotcom bubble bursting spread beyond the technology stocks, and markets around the world slumped. I was very glad all I had done with the money so far was pay off the mortgage, the credit cards, and the HP agreement on Moira's car. I had also spent £80k on a Mercedes S500: for the past 10 years I had been driving the car James McAdam had let me keep when he sacked me. Getting rid of it was a symbolic moment.

There was a very good reason why I hadn't been tempted by a portfolio of funds on the market: I already knew exactly what I was going to do with the money. I was going back into the jewellery business. One of the members who had joined the Work Shop was an old friend of mine called Jurek Piasecki. We had met several times when I was at Ratners and he had been the chairman of Goldsmiths, Britain's second largest jeweller. He was a rival as well, of course, but given our job titles we had always got on well. As the due diligence on the buy out had gone on so long, most of the members had found out I was leaving, and Jurek came up to me one day and asked what I was going to do with my money.

'Pay off my debts.'

'And after that?'

'Not sure.'

'I think you should go back into the jewellery business. No one's really started selling jewellery online yet. You could do that.'

'Are you mad? Go back into the one industry where my name stinks more than any other industry?'

'I know your name stinks…'

'You're not supposed to agree with me.'

'But it's a fact, and I think it could work to your advantage.'

'You've got to be kidding.'

'Listen, there are 60 million websites out there that nobody ever visits. With your name, there are people who will visit just out of curiosity. And if your prices were competitive enough…'

He didn't have to finish.

The wonderful thing about the success of the Work Shop was that it gave me the confidence to think he might be right. I had bounced back. I could hold my head up and walk into City institutions and raise finance. I had credibility. I wasn't just the idiot who'd made that speech any more. Jurek was on to something, and I knew that I was about to embark on another adventure in business.

I discussed Jurek's suggestion with Gary. It didn't seem like the best time to be launching a dotcom – they were folding left, right, and centre – and I wasn't sure we'd be able to raise the money. Gary then talked to a couple of people he knew, and when he got some positive feedback, I started to take the idea very seriously.

The first person I wanted onboard was Jurek himself. I still felt like a leper in the jewellery world, and I knew having the chairman of Goldsmiths behind me would make the wider industry take me seriously. Jurek said he would get Goldsmiths to do the fulfilment for me – i.e. sending out the orders – using their distribution network. This was exactly what I needed to hear, as it meant I could start the new business with a lot less cash.

Gary and I put together a proposal to take to potential investors. We went to see countless banks and venture capital firms, but I can't tell you how uninterested they were in putting their money into an online jeweller. 'People didn't want to buy jewellery from you in 1991, what makes you think they want their diamond rings to arrive in a Ratners box now?'

It was a fair question, so I tailored the business to be much more of a branded watch seller. If I could undercut the high street by 30% on watches by companies like Seiko, Accurist, and even Rolex, I didn't think that my reputation would have any influence on my customers' decisions. The banks didn't agree, and time after time we left with nothing more than a handshake and their best wishes. Despite my personal confidence in starting another business, I had to wonder if online jewellery would be it.

The press had been very interested in the rumours that I was going back into jewellery and there had been a fair bit of coverage. Word had obviously got out to the right people, and out of the blue I got a phone call from a company called SB&T in Bombay that specialised in set gemstones. They were coming to Britain and asked if I'd like to meet their managing director, Varij Sethi. I said of course.

They already had a big presence in America and the Middle East, but had so far been turned down by British retailers. When we met, I casually mentioned that we didn't just intend to sell through our website, but that we had ambitions to push merchandise through TV shopping channels, and Varij's eyes lit up. He was convinced that TV shopping was the best way to sell more jewellery, and on the basis that we would pursue the TV market aggressively, he agreed to part fund our launch to the tune of £2 million.

With SB&T and Goldsmiths behind me, raising the remainder of the money would be straightforward. What wasn't straightforward, however, was the name of the new company. The obvious name was Ratners Online, but none of us were sure if this would be a good thing or a bad thing. So we commissioned some market research to find out if my name still had negative associations, and I was stunned when we got the results. When members of the British public were asked to name a jeweller, the first name most of them gave was Ratners, a firm that hadn't been selling jewellery for 10 years. Many people hadn't noticed that Ratners had quietly slipped away from the high street. This meant that there were probably many people looking for jewellery online and putting my name into search engines. Finally, my name was going to be good for something; but when this was announced as our new company name in the press, I received a letter from Theodore Goddard, the solicitor I had used when I was at Ratners. He still worked for Signet and informed me that his client owned the Ratners name. I couldn't believe it, I didn't even own my own name!

Signet had spent the past 10 years distancing itself from the R word: it had shut all the shops and removed any trace of it from their corporate literature. Surely if I started trading under my own name again, nothing would make it clearer that they were a separate company? So I decided to fight for the right to use my own name, partly because I was just so angry with them because they hadn't just put in the letter that I couldn't use the Ratners name, they had gone as far as to say that they didn't think I had much chance of making a success of the venture. 'People like to feel and hold jewellery before they buy.' Of course, this just made me even more determined to make a success of the company, whatever we ended up calling it.

Gary and I took some legal advice on the best way to win the right to the Ratners name, and in the end we had to make a tough decision not to fight for it. There was a chance we would win the case, possibly even a good chance as they hadn't been using the name for so long, but there was enough of a chance that we wouldn't, and we just couldn't afford to lose. The money we had raised was all allocated to building our website, and on marketing and stock – any money for a legal battle would have to come out of mine and Gary's own pockets, and we just didn't have the cash. We made the decision to call our website geraldonline.com instead.

Although it should be possible to have an idea for an internet venture, get a website built by some teenage genius in their bedroom over a weekend, and launch it within a week, the truth is, building and testing a complex e-commerce website takes time. We couldn't afford any technical glitches, and at each level of testing, the site was refined and refined until it was ready for launch.

Much of the time, the technical staff could have been talking Chinese to me given how much I understood. But after hanging around with them for several months, certain things began to make sense, and I felt I had a pretty good grounding in the fundamentals of e-commerce.

All in all, raising the money, building the website, and hiring the staff took over two years. I suppose if I hadn't been comfortably off financially, I would have driven the pace of progress a little harder, but equally I knew I couldn't afford to launch with anything less than a polished website. I had to be absolutely sure our secure payments system wouldn't fail, that our delivery fulfilment would be flawless, and that our stock ordering was seamless: any tiny piece of negative publicity could kill us before we got started.

As I've always said, the jewellery business is about Christmas, so we planned our launch for early November 2004 to cash in on the surge in seasonal trade. We had a bit of publicity when we launched – it wasn't much, but it was enough to get three million hits in our first week. I must confess, I didn't really know what 'hits' were and for a brief moment I thought it meant visitors. Once I had the technology explained to me – a 'hit' is recorded every time a visitor views a piece of information, whether that's a photo or a piece of text – I realised that we had still had tens of thousands of visitors, which for our first week was unbelievable. Actual sales were slow at first, but I wasn't too worried: I knew how jewellery worked, and it was to be expected that customers would take their time to decide on a gift. They'd probably want to do some comparison shopping on the high street before they clicked on the 'buy' button.

However, towards the end of November, our number of visitors started to tail off, so I asked our PR agency to get us some coverage in the press. 'I don't care what they want me to do, but if they mention geraldonline.com, I'll do it.' After a week, the PR agent promised she had called every newspaper and magazine in the country, but hadn't been able to place a decent-sized story about us.

'I don't understand. When I announced I was going back into the jewellery trade, I got loads of coverage – and I didn't even have a website for people to look at then!'

'That's actually the problem Gerald. They all say they covered the story when you made the announcement. You going back into the jewellery business *was* the story. Hundreds of websites launch every week. I'm sorry, but it's just not news.'

It wasn't what I wanted to hear, but I knew it was the truth. And I also knew we were in serious trouble if we couldn't do something about it in the next couple of weeks: if we missed Christmas, the entire business was in jeopardy. And I didn't much like losing another fortune.

The obvious thing to do was to spend money on advertising. We were in an all-or-nothing situation, but a former employee from Ratners had launched an online jeweller the previous year. He had spent £3 million advertising on London buses and the underground, and he had still gone under. To make an impact at Christmas when all the big retailers are spending most of their annual marketing budget on big TV campaigns, I reckoned we'd need £30 million to get noticed. There was no way we could get our hands on that kind of money, so it wasn't even an option.

I can't remember who suggested calling Max Clifford, but I felt like I didn't have too many options. It was December 3rd and I only had a fortnight left to make the sales that would save my company. I looked him up in the phone book and dialled his number.

Max is probably the best known PR man in the country. If there's a big tabloid scandal, the chances are that he's either broken the story, or the celebrity who's been exposed will very quickly call Max and ask him to restore their public image. People tend to love him or loathe him, and usually it's the people who have never met him who have taken a dislike to him. I had no idea what to expect from him, but I was very impressed that when I called him at 2.30pm, he said he could see me immediately.

'I'll get there as soon as I can.'

I hadn't been expecting that kind of response, and so I wasn't even dressed for a meeting. I turned up on his doorstep looking a little dishevelled and telling him my business was about to go under. My appearance must have backed up my story, and he got straight on the phone to his contacts. While I was sitting there, he arranged interviews with the *Sun* and the *Mirror*, the two papers that had done me so much damage 12 years before. He was obviously owed some favours and he called them in for me. It made me wish I had hired him after I had made the speech.

Obviously the journalists dragged up all of the coverage about the speech again, and I had to fall on my sword so many times I looked like Swiss cheese, but it gave them a story, and it gave geraldonline.com the coverage it needed. In the next week, Max had me on a seemingly endless tour of TV and radio studios, taking part in panel shows, and being interviewed on breakfast telly.

It's a fact of life, and business, that deals are done between people who like each other, and it was clear that Max was getting journalists to write about me so that at some future date they would be offered a much juicier story. He was also clearly on first name terms with Rebekah Wade, the editor of the *Sun* and one of the most powerful people in the country. If she could be persuaded that geraldonline.com was a story, then the rest of the media was a pushover. The relationship between Max and Rebekah probably rescued my business, because in the following days, our figures started to climb dramatically. I don't think I'm the only one who sees the irony in the press being responsible for my rehabilitation when they had been so instrumental in my downfall.

I had been paying my previous PR agency – a specialist corporate agency with lots of big City clients – £3000 a month and it was a waste of money. I paid Max Clifford £10,000 a month, and it was arguably the best money I have ever spent. On the back of the tabloid exposure, the broadsheets starting talking to me again, and I had the most fabulous coverage. Not just little gossip pieces, but double-page spreads with photos of lots of our products.

Max had also arranged for me to have copy approval, which meant I could edit out anything I didn't like. I would go to bed on a Sunday night unable to sleep because I was so excited about a piece that I knew would appear on Monday morning saying 'because of his connections with India, he is able to undercut the high street by 40 per cent'. It was dynamite, and I knew it would encourage not just visits, but purchases.

Max wasn't perfect though. He had arranged for me to do an interview on LBC radio in London. I was driving into their studio in West London and listening to the station when I heard a trailer for my interview. *Coming up in the next half hour, we've got Gerald Ratner, the man who said his jewellery was crap...* I was so furious, and so tired of explaining that I had NEVER said my jewellery was crap, that I phoned up the station from my mobile and said I was turning my car around.

They were very apologetic and persuaded me to go on air anyway, where I'd be given all the time I needed to tell my side of the story. I relented, and when I got to the studio, the researcher handed me a press release from Max Clifford. It said that I had called my jewellery crap. If my own PR couldn't get it right, I couldn't really blame the press if they kept getting it wrong.

CHAPTER 27

Thinking Big

The great thing about running a business online is that you can track how your customers use your site. You can see if there are certain things that often get bought as a package – like a necklace and earrings – or a product that often gets left in shopping baskets without the customer making it to the checkout. Analysing your website's statistics allows you to see your business how your customers see it, and with constant monitoring and tweaking, you can very quickly grow an effective business.

It was very interesting for me personally going back into the industry after a long break and seeing just how much had changed. People were spending more money on individual items than they had done in the Nineties: at Ratners, our average ticket price had been £30; at geraldonline.com it is over £200. Fashion had also changed, and the gold chains and bracelets that had been the staple of the jewellery business in the Eighties were out and bling was in. The chunkier the gold and the more numerous the gemstones, the easier it was to shift as customers copied rappers and R&B culture. I was surprised to find out just how many of our customers were men. I guess I can thank David Beckham's earrings for that.

In the Eighties, it had been enough to say that a chain was gold: most of our customers didn't care if it was 9ct or 18ct, and a small diamond was as saleable as a big one if the price was right. Online,

different, and it's very easy for customers to compare our
with our competitors'. That's part of the reason why I had
anti.. .ted that we would do very well on watch sales: with my contacts I had secured some deals from old friends that meant we would
be the cheapest on the market with big brand watches. But what I
hadn't realised is that the internet also allows shoppers to compare
jewellery too. These days, when people buy a diamond ring online,
they're looking for evidence that they're buying quality, and so retailers issue certificates guaranteeing the 4 Cs – cut, colour, clarity, and
carat – so customers can compare. We were offering certified gems at
the best prices, and I was surprised to find that our gem sales easily
outstripped our watch sales. And of course, I did what I've always
done: give the customer what they want. This meant removing lines
that weren't selling well, promoting lines we knew had wide appeal,
and making sure that our big sellers were always in stock.

The internet has completely changed the way people buy jewellery.
No one ever came into a branch of Ratners in the Seventies or Eighties
and asked about the clarity of our gemstones. Certainly no one ever
asked for a certified stone. But now that research is so easy online, it
has become key in helping buyers identify quality products. The other
thing that's changed, of course, is the ethical element. Most buyers
today insist that their diamonds shouldn't be 'conflict diamonds', i.e.
stones from places like Sierra Leone where diamonds are mined to
fund wars. No one had ever heard of a conflict diamond in the Eighties.
I found it fascinating that so much had changed in the business in a
relatively short space of time.

That's not to say that price isn't still absolutely crucial, and thanks to
SB&T, geraldonline.com can sell very high-quality diamond jewellery
at remarkable prices. I found rings and earrings in the UK that retailed
for £1000 and asked SB&T to make copies of them. They were able to
produce stunning replicas so cheaply that we could sell them for £590.
With those kinds of discounts, we did very well on price comparison
websites like Pricerunner and Kelkoo, and that's how we found a lot
of our customers. We also – surprisingly, in my view – discovered that

we couldn't find a market for Pulsar and Accurist watches when our discount was only £20 below the high street. Unless the discount was substantial, buyers would still prefer to go to the high street and feel it on their wrist before they bought.

When I left Ratners, the idea that people would buy jewellery through their TV sounded like something out of science fiction, but TV sales are now a very important part of our business. We act as wholesalers for SB&T in the UK, and Varij was right to be excited about selling his products on TV, partly because jewellery looks so good on TV and partly because there are a lot of women watching at home who buy treats for themselves. Gary is actually the one who goes on TV and talks about our products: his creative accounting isn't his only artistic talent.

The internet has rewritten the rules of how to run a business. In the Eighties and Nineties, there was a formality to corporate structures, and it was a status thing to have so many people working for you. These days, job titles and staff numbers are no longer anything to brag about, and in smaller, sleeker organisations, people just get on with their jobs without getting sidetracked by unnecessary corporate bullshit. In some ways, it's a lot like the early days of Ratners with Mr Hussein working in a tiny office on his own doing the work of 10 men. Computer systems mean we don't need an entire finance department, and as we don't have thousands of shops, we don't need a facilities team eating into our profits. I don't have a team of staff running around after me – the days of a chauffeur and a PA have long gone – and I answer my own emails and manage stock levels from a laptop in my garden.

It's a very nice way to work, and although my kids are getting a bit too old to need their dad around all the time, there is still one member of the family who needs a lot of hands-on attention: our chocolate brown Labrador Alfie. While I've been writing this, he's been staring at me, demanding to be fed and walked. Although he's a bit of a pain, he's an adorable dog who hasn't got a nasty streak in his body.

When I take him for a walk, the neighbours greet him and ignore me. I'm just 'Alfie's dad'. When he was a puppy, he would escape and because he's so adorable, the neighbours used to feed him. I couldn't blame them: when Alfie wants food he can be incredibly persuasive. He's a very smart dog and always seems to understand what we're talking about. Some days, I would get more done if I went into the office.

Because I run a very sleek and responsive organisation, we can be extremely competitive and respond to changes in fashion extraordinarily quickly. This has allowed us to build a very successful business in a short space of time, and we have become Britain's biggest online jewellery retailer.

Obviously, I've benefited because the internet has grown so much since our launch three years ago, and by and large, making geraldonline. com a success has been relatively easy, compared with the battles I fought at Ratners. All I've done is look at the competition – which was mostly American sites when we launched – and copied what worked best, and then sourced the best products and offered them at the best prices. It's really not that different from the days when I copied Terry's and Robert Anthony's shops. There have been a few glitches – like the day in December 2006 when our servers went down because we had too much Christmas traffic – and problems with fraud (we get targeted by fraudsters using stolen credit cards as gems have such a high resale value), but for most of the week, I don't even need to visit our warehouse and just answer emails from home.

Being back in control of a successful company has meant that journalists started to phone me up for quotes for stories they were doing about the jewellery business. Early in 2006, one of those calls came from the *Daily Telegraph* who wanted to know what I thought of the rumours that Signet would bid for Zales' American operation.

'I think it's a sign that they probably intend to concentrate on their successful American shops', I said, stopping short of adding that it was only because of me that they had those profitable shops in the first place.

'And if that meant that they were going to dispose of their UK shops, would you be interested in buying them?'

'Well, that's a very interesting idea.'

'Is that a yes then?'

'I suppose it is.'

Needless to say, the next day, the *Telegraph* ran a piece saying that I was eyeing up a takeover of the old family business. Apart from the fact that I didn't have the money to do such a thing, it seemed like quite a plausible proposition. Signet was doing well in the States because it was being run by Nate Lite's son and the people I had left in charge there. At the time, it looked like their profits were propping up the UK side of things, which in my view had been mismanaged since my departure. And when McAdam left and was replaced by a new chief executive who was an American, it didn't take a maths genius to add two and two and get five: it seemed the logical thing for them to ditch their UK operation and concentrate on their strengths.

Not long after the *Telegraph* hit the streets, I got a call from my old accountant at BDO Stoy Hayward. He had handled my tax returns for 35 years and he knew I didn't have the necessary cash to mount a bid.

'If you're serious about it Gerald, we have a merchant bank division that could help you.'

'I think I'm going to need all the help I can get.'

With BDO's help, I was eventually introduced to a venture capitalist who was willing to finance a bid. With deals of that size, you need to do a certain amount of due diligence even before you put your bid in, so we asked Signet if we could see their accounts. We got a letter back saying that they would not give us access, and that effectively stopped me in my tracks.

I firmly believe that they want to sell the business, but I think I am the last person in the world they want to sell to. They would see it as a retrograde step and it would just be too embarrassing for them. By making my intentions public, I backed them into a corner and the only thing they could do to save face was say no.

It would give me a huge amount of pleasure to buy back the UK shops Signet still owns. You just have to look in H. Samuel's windows to see why they are not performing as they should be, and as time goes on and if the shops perform badly, then I think Signet will be forced to sell. I might be getting on a bit, but I can wait, and I think that's the big difference between me in 1987 and me in 2007: I've learnt the art of patience. If they ever put those shops up for sale, I will certainly be one of the bidders.

My immediate concern is to make geraldonline.com even bigger and more profitable. Our next move will be to sell premium watches from Cartier and Rolex, but as these brands don't like to be associated with discount retailers, I will have to buy them on the grey market from intermediaries who can sell them to me at cost plus 5%. This enables me to sell to the public at as much as 20% below the high street, saving customers thousands of pounds on the more exclusive items.

It won't just be the profit we make on the watches that will help grow the business, as I know from owning Ernest Jones that when you put a Rolex in your shop window, the diamond ring next to it suddenly looks a lot more desirable. We only sold Rolexes in 80 of our Ernest Jones shops, and it was those 80 shops that sold the most diamond rings.

I think it's crucial that we bring the really big names onto our website, but unfortunately that means I have had to part company with Goldsmiths, as my buying watches on the grey market would mean Rolex and Cartier would terminate their arrangements with Goldsmiths. I will, of course, always be incredibly grateful to Jurek for helping me at the beginning, and for suggesting online retailing in the first place.

We now manage our own fulfilment from our well-stocked warehouse in Oxfordshire, and we get some very nice emails from customers who are amazed that they can order something at 2 o'clock in the afternoon and it arrives as promised the following morning in a lovely box. The fulfilment side of the business is the most expensive, in terms of manpower and premises, and is a cost we almost certainly couldn't have shouldered at launch. As I say, I am very grateful to Jurek.

I have learnt that you can't predict the course a business will take, but if my plans for geraldonline.com come off, then the next few years will be very exciting. In fact, the only thing I know for sure is that I won't be retiring. I was forced into early retirement at 41 and hated it, so I think I shall probably work until I drop. I can't understand why people want to move to a little house in Cornwall, watch TV all day, and meet the same people in the pub every evening. But then, they don't run the country's biggest online jeweller.

I have discussed with the other directors where we might take geraldonline.com in the next couple of years. One possibility we've discussed is a flotation. Although it would be wonderful to take the profits from my investment, I'm not sure how I feel about going back to being at the mercy of brokers and analysts. I wish I could say that I would handle the pressure totally differently, but I have a sense that my competitive streak wouldn't need much encouragement: the desire to talk up my figures would be too tempting and I could get caught up in another cycle of expansion and stretching to meet forecasts.

If history was to repeat itself, I suppose if nothing else it would provide a good ending for *Ratner the Musical*! I still can't quite believe it, but I was approached by Simon Nye, the writer of *Men Behaving Badly*, a few years ago saying he wanted to write a musical about my life. I thought he was joking of course – I was told the first line was 'I had it all in my lap, until I said the word crap!' – but after meeting him I realised he was serious. He's working with Howard Goodall, who wrote the music for Blackadder among other things, and I've been told the BBC have commissioned it.

They don't need my permission to use my story, and I certainly won't get any money from it, but it's pretty surreal to find yourself not just in random lists of great mistakes, but the subject of a musical. Still, at least it will be good publicity for geraldonline.com.

CHAPTER 28

What Goes Around

I had an idea for a publicity stunt a couple of years ago while I was out cycling. What if I went back to the IOD and made another speech? geraldonline.com wasn't getting a lot of coverage at the time, and I thought my return to the IOD would be irresistible for journalists. So I wrote to the Institute and asked them if they would invite me back. They agreed, and I took to the stage again at one of their events in 2005.

Rather than give a speech, I was asked to do a question and answer session with their chief executive. When my name was announced they played that song by Chumbawumba with the lyrics *I get knocked down, but I get up again*, and that seemed to set the tone for the whole session. I was introduced as the man who had run a company with a billion pounds worth of sales, profits of £125 million, 2500 shops and 27,000 staff... until I went to the IOD. This also got a laugh. And when I was asked if I'd considered suicide, I replied that, 'as Joan Rivers once said, suicide is so Eighties', and this got even more applause.

The following day, I got a flurry of emails from people saying how much they had enjoyed the session, and one of them was from a man who was arranging a convention for ABTA and said I was exactly the kind of speaker he'd like to put on the programme. The convention was in Marrakech, and he wanted to know if I was interested. Needless to say, Moira and I had a lovely long weekend in Morocco – all expenses paid – and I even got a cheque at the end of it.

When I got home, someone who'd been at the ABTA conference wondered if I'd give the same speech to a timeshare organisation. I couldn't quite believe I'd get paid again for giving the same speech. No research, no rehearsals, all I had to do was turn up. I said yes again. In 2006, I said yes over 100 times and unexpectedly found myself with a new career: public speaking.

Several of the events I'm asked to talk at are for bankruptees and insolvent traders. Every year, thousands of businesses fail, and for every business that stops trading there's someone who has lost everything. I don't just mean their money, but they've lost their status, often their marriage, their direction. They've also lost hope, and the most important thing I do at these speeches is turn up. Just seeing someone recover from the most spectacular failure anyone's ever heard of gives them hope to know that anyone can bounce back.

Obviously it took me a long time to claw my way back, but what I now call my 'wilderness years' gave me a chance to recuperate. I really believe now that if you've been through a terrible experience, you have to get your head straight before you can do anything else. You need to be able to start your next venture with a clean slate, and if that means taking a sabbatical, or travelling around the world, then that's OK: you can't recover from a failed business – and all the pain that places on every part of your life – overnight. You've got to start afresh, and that means dealing with whatever baggage you are carrying. It's no good being angry or blaming anyone else. I could have lain in bed at night plotting how I'd wreak revenge on James McAdam for firing me. But that wouldn't have been productive, and I gradually came to accept that I had been unlucky. No more, no less, just unlucky, and there's a certain kind of peace that comes with accepting bad luck.

I can usually tell who in my audiences has just lost their business and who is a couple of months down the line. Those who have only just gone under are far more restless and full of 'I'll show you', but all their rage is stopping them from getting their head straight. I tell them: 'You've been successful once, you just need to work out what made you successful and you will succeed again.' It's simple advice, but it took me a decade to work it out. I also tell them that failure has its upside: they'll never be worried about being seen in the right bar, or getting the best seat on the plane any more because failure teaches you that none of that matters.

Apart from the fact that I enjoy these speeches – in many ways, it's actually been quite cathartic – it has been a very nice source of income. In the early days of geraldonline.com, it meant I didn't need to draw a salary from the business, which meant the money could be spent getting the company where I wanted it to be. I do quite a few speeches for charity, but I usually charge and I can get up to £5000 for each event. It's a lot of money for what is sometimes only a few hours work – and I'm only on the C list. B listers, I'm told, get twice that, and A listers often get £40,000 for a night. My ambition for the next year is to become a B lister!

I get an enormous buzz out of public speaking, and I've got to meet some great people – often other entrepreneurs I've seen on TV – who I would otherwise never meet. I travel all over the country, and all over the world, and I've realised that audiences really respond to someone who's made a mistake. Organisers tell me that audiences learn more from me than some guy with the Midas touch who doesn't appear to have any flaws.

Nine times out of ten, people start laughing in the first five minutes, but occasionally I bomb. Just like the old days, I know that if they laugh at the first joke, then they'll laugh for the rest of it. Ultimately it's quite an unusual story, how a businessman at the top of his game can lose it all so quickly over something so stupid. I'm sure that schadenfreude has something to do with people's interest in my downfall, but I think mostly people are interested in how you start again with less than zero. I guess I enjoy the speaking because it gives me a chance to show that Gerald Ratner isn't one of the 50 great mistakes in history. It's ironic, of course, that giving a speech once ruined me, and that in the past two years I guess you could say it has rescued me. And because of what happened, I don't even care that much if I say something stupid because I know that if I get knocked down, I'll get back up again.

The Speech

Transcript of my 1991 speech to The Institute of Directors - abridged for the Director Magazine convention issue

This has been a difficult recession. In previous recessions manufacturing took the brunt but this time the recession's main victims are high-street retailers. The recession is high-street led.

Now, as jewellery is a luxury purchase, you might think that we at Ratners would be suffering more than most – we're not. We are not on the crest of a wave either – but we *are* coping. And in fact this morning we announced record profits of £115m.

Eight years ago, the announcement we were making was that the company had just lost £350,000. So, before I talk about potential for the next eight years it's important to see how we have achieved this growth.

If there are any tips in my story that may be of help to you – please go ahead and use them. That is, as long as you don't diversify into the jewellery business!

The Ratner group is fundamentally a jewellery retailing operation with over 2,200 shops. One thousand are in the US and the rest are all in the UK.

We cover a number of brand names, with our major chains in the UK being Ratners, H Samuel, Zales and Watches of Switzerland.

The theme of today's conference is quality, choice and prosperity which, at least partially, links quite nicely with our businesses.

Zales, the diamond specialist of the group, represents quality. And H Samuel, which operates from larger units and carries bigger ranges including jewellery gifts – represents choice. Watches of Switzerland, which sells watches costing as much as £250,000, certainly represents prosperity.

That leaves me with the original Ratners chain – and I have to admit that while it offers choice with its 99p earrings, it is positioned very down-market, doesn't represent prosperity and, to be frank, has got very little to do with quality.

Also in Ratners we sell gifts as well as jewellery things like a tea pot for £2, or a coffee table book that doesn't open, complete with antique dust. We also do cut glass sherry decanters complete with six glasses on a silver-plated tray – that your butler can serve your drinks on – all for £4.95. People say how can you sell this for such a low price – I say because it's crap.

Our Ratners shops will never win any awards for design. They're not in the best possible taste and in fact some people say they can't even see the jewellery for all the posters and banners smothering the shop windows.

It's interesting that these shops, which everyone has a good laugh about, take more money per square foot than any other retailer in Europe.

Why? Because we give the customers what they want.

In our shops today, jewellery is bought largely on impulse – especially in Ratners and H Samuel. The look of the shops, with pop music playing, garish colours and bright lights is worlds apart from the old-fashioned jewellers.

Before 1984 Ratners was one of them. In those days nothing in the windows was priced. Today everything in our windows is clearly priced and clearly described.

The old jewellers used to lock the doors behind you, probably bolted them as well. Now when our shops are open, you'll see no doors, we take them away.

Before 1984 the average item in a jewellers shop cost over £300. Today in our shops it's no longer a luxury – it's about £20.

We even sell a pair of earrings for under £1, which some people say is cheaper than a prawn sandwich from Marks and Spencers, but I have to say the earrings probably won't last as long!

This year we introduced a range of men's earrings, also at 99p – but 99p each – which we thought was a great marketing ploy as the fashion for men is only to wear one. It doubles the profit margin!

By the way, I notice very few IOD male members wearing an earring. Hopefully you will become more fashion conscious by next year's convention.

So what we have done in our market is to throw out all the sacred rules and customs – however sanctified-by-time they were.

We've broken down the barriers put up by the jewellers who felt that prestige and mystique are what the public wants. The jeweller of old targeted a very small part of the population – the better off. Jewellery, like air travel or going out to eat, was always the province of the rich.

Today any young teenager can afford to pick up a piece of gold jewellery as a fashion accessory with a new outfit.

Our future success will come from continuing to offer the public what they want – not what we want to give them. What do people want these days? What do they want?

At the moment what they are looking for is new products. Somebody once did a survey and the most popular word that people looked for on their shopping travels was the word "new", and at Ratners whenever we have got anything new in we stick a label saying "new" on it.

So they want new and exciting products and then secondly they have got to have products that they can afford.

A lot of retailers (and this probably applies to other business people) are afraid to try anything new today – to beat this recession. They're trying to deal with this recession by walking away from it and hibernating. They hope to survive like hedgehogs in the winter by getting out of sight and hoping they are going to emerge totally unscathed and reborn when its all over.

That isn't going to work!

You can't do that in retailing anyway. Your shops and your staff – they'll all need you to be out there continuously with new products, new ideas, new promotions and different sorts of schemes.

Just because there's a recession, doesn't mean we can all stop.

Think of your business as a pet dog. You can't stop feeding it or stroking it, or taking it for walks because you're in hard times. What's going to happen if you don't feed your dog is that it's going to drop dead.

Well the same thing can easily happen to the business.

Yes, you've got to be sensible about things and try to help results by spending less, but business hibernation in recession means death. Death through stagnation.

Now, if there *is* one good thing about this recession, it is that you can now negotiate with people. So it is possible to cut overheads and costs.

But just as we want to save money when we're dealing with suppliers and shopfitters, our customers also want a bargain, or at least they want to think they're getting a bargain because of the recession.

They want to feel that they virtually steal something from you. And quite honestly, the only way that you can get people to buy anything in this climate is to make sure they know they've got a good deal.

Our offers are genuine. If they weren't, the customers would soon find out and leave us.

The easiest thing to do in this climate to combat this recession is to lower prices. But that doesn't get you anywhere!

If your margins go down – you'll suffer.

The answer is to get more out of your suppliers – or more out of them than you actually pass on to your customer in those deals. Which means close co-operation with them, discussing innovation and new design – and helping them achieve efficiency in production.

Right now, our customers not only want lower prices, but they also want free offers, something for nothing.

We are in the age of the value-added consumer. My wife is more interested in the gift she gets than the actual perfume itself. It's the "add-ons" that seem to count at the moment. The lowest ticket price on its own is just not enough to keep the pundits happy.

At Ratners we have successfully been running a voucher scheme. A £50 voucher if you spend £150. Now that might sound to you like a 33 per cent discount, which of course would be suicidal from our point of view.

In fact you'd be wrong, somebody spending £300 would still only get one voucher, so the average spend that qualified for a voucher would be around £200. This lowers the discount immediately from 33 per cent to 25 per cent.

But we are not handing out £50 notes. It's a voucher. That voucher cost us somewhere in the region of £25 because we make double-up margins – we don't give the stuff away. That brings it down to 12.5 per cent.

The customer cannot redeem the voucher immediately, so when they return they usually buy something costing more than £50. On average we get an additional tenner, which is not much but it's better than nothing.

That's an extra £5 profit which saves us a further 2.5 per cent. So now we're down to a ten per cent discount.

Some people lose their voucher or don't bother to redeem it. So we're now at nine per cent.

We also calculate that before vouchers, 25 per cent of our customers used to ask for a discount. Now they get a voucher instead, which reduces it by a further 2.5 per cent. So you end up with not 33 per cent but 6.5 per cent. That's good marketing!

And we found sales over £150 increased by more than 50 per cent over the Christmas period when we ran this promotion. So it turned out to be a very profitable promotion.

Now if you didn't follow all the details there, I don't mind a bit because I'd rather you worked out your own scheme anyway!

This Christmas we might trim the voucher to £25 and give it on things over £100, which will cost us even less.

But look what else we're giving the customers as well as the vouchers. Interest-free credit, free insurance, 30-day money back guarantee – if they change their mind they can have a full refund.

That's how confident we are about our prices.

With 34 per cent of the market you may wonder why we are trying so hard.

It's because we're not only competing with the other jewellers, but with everyone else in the high street for a shrinking disposable income. And how can any of our competitors, or any of the other jewellers, compete with that?

So this is Ratners' answer to the recession. Give the customers such a brilliant offer that they can't refuse it.

Yes, it's market trading. But have you ever seen a street market that is empty?

It is this approach – it's a simplistic approach – but it's this approach that has taken us from under two per cent of the market to 34 per cent of the jewellery spending today. (I hope there is nobody from the monopolies commission here!)

Of course, there are other things we have going for us – a very speedy stock replacement system, for example. It's essential when somebody comes into the shop, that we actually have the item they want. I know it's obvious, but it's crucial.

And then it's important that we motivate our staff. Our staff are all on incentive schemes where they earn more money based on what they sell.

But what has really made the difference for us was that we took the mystique out of jewellery. We market it like baked beans or like anything else and we probably market it even more aggressively.

Aggressive marketing has to be carried out all the time but it is not the only action to be taken – particularly during a recession. We also have to manage costs.

You must make your operation lean. No-one likes reducing staff; we certainly don't. It means hardship for the people we make redundant but unfortunately, if business is tight, it is sometimes unavoidable.

I believe, however, that it's better, to reduce the number of your staff than the money that they are paid.

The recession is a challenge to them and you want to keep the people who can respond to that challenge. So we try not to reduce pay or privileges for our existing staff.

In addition to managing cost we also have to manage the group's liquidity – we have successfully implemented a major reduction in stock and we make sure today that we only buy what we sell.

We do not carry excess stock in the warehouse. This is achieved by monitoring sales on a daily basis – the just-in-time approach.

But all of our controls and cost-cutting are done in a manner to ensure that they won't affect sales. Whatever we're redoing, we communicate with our staff, we have frequent meetings with our managers, getting their opinion and telling them our strategies.

One question we ask ourselves constantly is: "What we are going to do once we hit our 50 per cent target?" Could we transport our formula to the Continent or the US? Otherwise we would get into the law of diminishing returns.

In the UK, the jewellery market has grown faster than any other sector in the high street and that's mainly because we have made it more affordable and more fashionable – and more high profile.

When we did consider the Continent we had one advantage – we'd already been there.

Ratners had expanded into Europe – back in the seventies. We'd opened about half a dozen shops in the summer of 1974 – in Holland – and they actually did quite well that summer.

The problem was when Christmas came around and the figures didn't go up. We discovered that they don't celebrate Christmas in Holland and they don't give Christmas presents. And as 90 per cent of jewellers' profits are made in December, that was a slight drawback – to say the least.

Perhaps this is an extreme example of not researching your market before you go in, of not looking before you leap. But that is the sort of mistake that is going to be made again in 1992.

And it isn't enough to research new markets, you've got to know your market. We know the jewellery market in the UK pretty well. We don't know everything about it, but we think we know more than our competitors and that's the only basis on which you can be successful in any market.

We decided to go to the US before Europe, as this is the second largest market for jewellery in the world, after Japan. It's a market worth $22bn – five times the size of the UK jewellery market.

So, in the US we acquired a chain, which appropriately was called Sterling. We decided it was the best jewellery retailer in the US – it wasn't the biggest, just the best.

Because rents in the US are linked to sales you can actually find out who is taking the most money. You can find out what every trader is taking. The mall owners are quite happy to tell you that. They don't do it over here because sales are not linked to rents and they don't know.

So as we travelled around the malls, without any exception Sterling was taking more money than any other jeweller. That is useful information to know when you're buying a business.

So at that point we arranged to visit their head office. We also found their gross margins – it's no good just taking sales if they're not making the profit margins – we found that their gross margins were 61 per cent, also the highest in the trade.

Their bad debt write-off was, and is, the lowest in the trade and this is totally crucial as far as the US is concerned, where everybody wants to buy everything on credit.

All of this, plus first-class management.

In the four years since we bought the business we've never regretted it. We have used their proven methods, we have built on their foundations and we have expanded their operation tenfold from 100 to 1,000 shops.

Last year we made $110m in the US – more than any UK retailer has *ever* achieved there. And we know that this was due to the fact that we weren't arrogant enough to try and transport our formula – however successful it was in the UK – straight across to the US. We got local management to deal with it and that's the secret.

We've had criticism on the way. We bought Kays in America last year, a chain of 500 shops. The City analysts gave it the thumbs down. The press unanimously condemned it. There were even calls from the institution for us to appoint non-executive directors to join our board, and our shares halved in price.

Apart from all that, it was pretty well received.

But the thing that none of them yet understand is that just like all our previous acquisitions in the US (and we've done four or five and they've all been successful), Kays will be totally transformed, converted to the successful Sterling formula.

It worked for our previous acquisitions and its already working, I'm glad to say, for Kays.

So we have used the eighties to expand our businesses. We've taken full advantage of the economic climate.

In the nineties we are capitalising on our position.

So to sum up. Whether we are in the US or the UK or on the Continent of Europe – whether we're in recession or in boom – we will carry on being prosperous by taking market share.

To do this we will continue to offer value for money; that's central.

We must go on offering the widest possible choice, from the best locations, operated by staff who know what they are doing and who are fully trained.

We must give the best service and project the highest possible quality standards.

In other words we must show the customer that if they want jewellery, we're the place to come to. We're the only real choice that they've got. We are what the Americans call "category killers."

The nineties are certainly going to be tough for all of us. Everyone agrees about that. There'll be more losers than winners.

The winners will be the ones that can control costs without losing innovation. The winners will be the ones that can find a way of blending the two. We are totally determined that the winners will include Ratners.

We share the recession together, and I hope that before long we will also share good times. Good luck for you, your staff and your companies.

(*Reproduced with permission of The Institute of Directors*).

Index